The Sales Funnel Book

How To Multiply Your Business With Marketing Automation

Nathan Williams

Copyright

First Printing: 2016

ISBN-13: 978-1540488091

ISBN-10: 1540488098

Crazy Eye Media, LLC

PO Box 2871

Chester, VA 23831

https://crazyeyemarketing.com

Disclaimers

Limit of Liability / Disclaimer of Warranty

While the publisher and author have used their best efforts in preparing this book, they make no representations or warranties regarding the accuracy or completeness of the contents of this book. The publisher and author specifically disclaim any implied warranties of merchantability or fitness for a particular purpose, and make no guarantees whatsoever that you will achieve any particular result. Any case studies that are presented herein do not necessarily represent what you should expect to achieve, since business success depends on a variety of factors. We believe all case studies and results presented herein are true and accurate, but we have not audited the results. The advice and strategies contained in the book may not even be suitable for your situation, and you should consult your own advisors as appropriate. The publisher and author shall not be held liable for any loss of profit or any other commercial damages, including but not limited to special, incidental, consequential, or other damages. The fact that an organization or website is referred to in this work as a citation and/or a potential source of information does not mean that the publisher or author endorses the information the organization or website may provide or the recommendations it may make. Further, readers should be aware that Internet websites listed in this work may have changed or disappeared after this work was written.

Earnings Disclaimer

We don't believe in get rich programs – all human progress and accomplishment takes hard work. As stipulated by law, we cannot and do not make any guarantees about your ability to get results or earn any money with your ideas, information, tools, or strategies. After all, it takes hard work to succeed in any type of business. Nothing in this book or any of our websites is a promise or guarantee of results or future earnings, and we do not offer any legal, medical, tax, or other professional advice. Any financial numbers referenced here, or on any of our sites, are simply estimates or projections, and should not be considered exact, actual, or as a promise of potential earnings – all numbers are illustrative only.

Table Of Contents

Preface

A sales funnel is the visual representation of how businesses acquire leads, convert them into customers, and increase customer lifetime value.

As you're well aware, these three areas are complex.

There are a million ways to acquire leads.

A million ways to convert leads into customers.

And a million ways to increase customer lifetime value.

Thus, **a sales funnel is an incredibly complex system**.

This guidebook is my best attempt to provide you with a strategic framework to reference when building your sales funnels.

How I "See" A Sales Funnel

The phrase "sales funnel" gets thrown around **a lot**.

Everyone calls *everything* a sales funnel.

There's a funnel for this and a funnel for that.

There are pre-built funnels and tools to help you build funnels in less than 10 minutes.

This is all fine and dandy.

I find myself calling everything a funnel as well because every time you're doing these three things …

1) Capturing leads
2) Converting leads into customers
3) Increasing customer lifetime value

... you're essentially making a sales funnel.

However, on a large scale ...

*I see a sales funnel **AS** your business.*

It's not some random "thing" you have sitting over there in the corner.

It's not something you just kinda "do" when you feel like it.

It's not just sending emails.

It's not just editing the order flow.

It encompasses all your products and services and how they're connected so you can increase customer lifetime value via up-sells, down-sells, and cross-sells.

It encompasses all your ads, pages, emails, direct mailings, text messages, videos, content, etc.

It's a lot.

I don't say all this to scare you or make you feel overwhelmed *(that would be bad if I scared you away in the first couple pages!)*.

I say this to give you a frame of reference.

I want you to "see" the sales funnel from a 30,000-foot view.

I want you to think bigger than simply setting up a "book funnel" that sells your book, a course, and coaching.

Or a webinar funnel that sells your high-end coaching service with a down-sell of a self-guided course.

Think bigger.

Think about **everything** you offer.

Think about what you can offer to fill any gaps.

Think about how it's all connected.

What's a good up-sell? Down-sell? Cross-sell?

How do you, and can you, deliver more value to your audience?

Speaking of your audience, think about them ... *all of them* ... they're all different.

They all have different motivators, personalities, hobbies, and interests.

Now, how are you going to connect everything you offer to the specific interests and requirements of your audience?

The Interest Driven Sales Funnel.

The Interest Driven Sales Funnel

The Interest Driven Sales Funnel

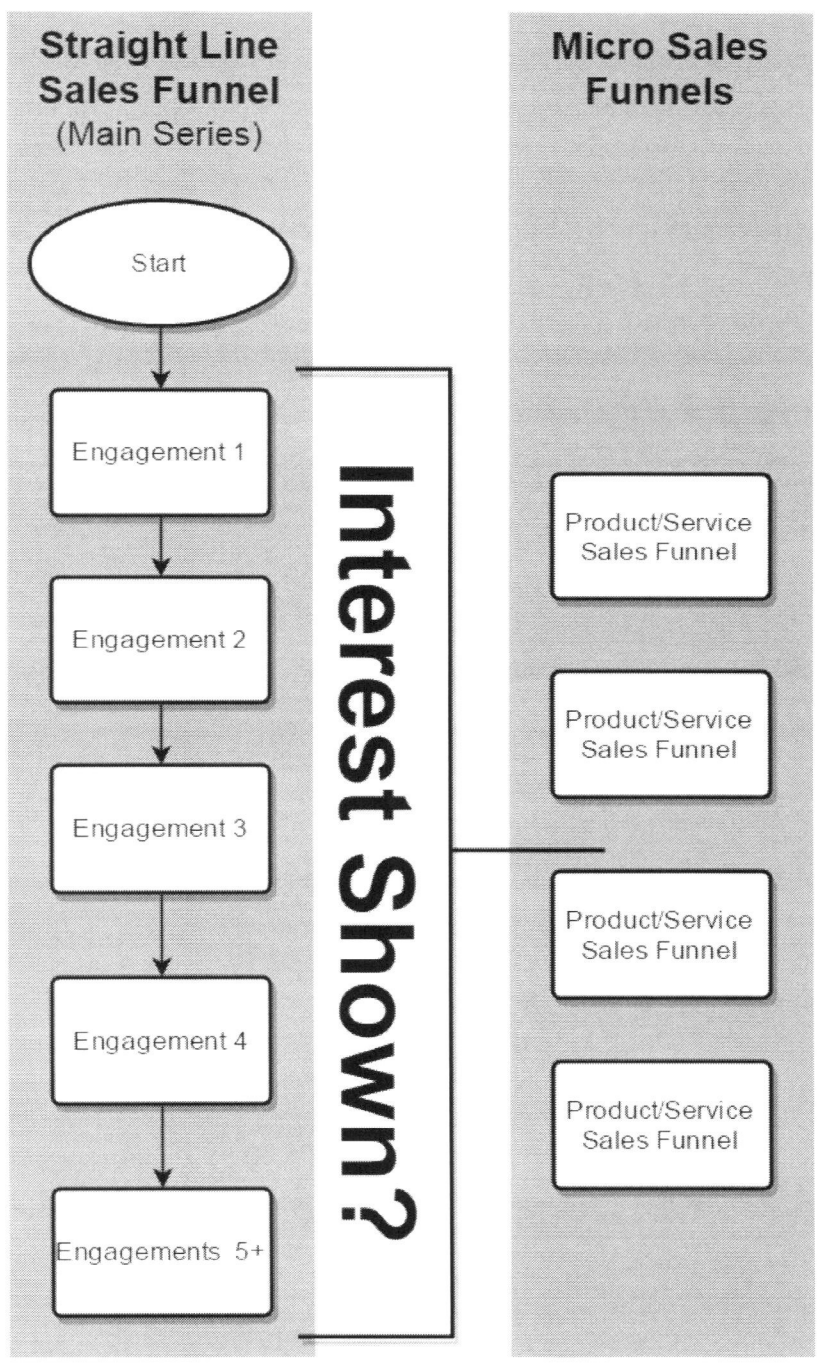

General Concept

You're going to engage your audience many times, from many angles, with many offers; this is the general concept of the Interest Driven Sales Funnel.

This is represented on the left hand side of the diagram by the Straight Line Sales Funnel or Main Series.

Whenever one of our engagements resonates with an audience member (an interest is shown), we move them into one of our Micro Sales Funnels or Product/Service Sales Funnels.

The Micro Sales Funnels are what you likely think of when you hear the phrase "sales funnel".

The Micro Sales Funnels are the up-sell funnels, book funnels, webinar funnels, product launch funnels, etc. you always hear about.

The goal of the Micro Sales Funnel is to sell a product or service the individual has shown interest in.

We'll delve into much greater detail of these funnels later in this guidebook, but first I want to give you a few examples.

Huge Benefits

The first benefit of the Interest Driven Sales Funnel is that it allows your audience to **self-segment**.

You don't have to place individuals into different segments you *"think"* are right. Instead, you **know** what segments people need to be in because they put themselves in the appropriate segment(s) based on their actions.

Picture it "adapting" to each individual subscriber. It automatically figures out what they like and proceeds to only show them what they want to see.

The second massive benefit of the Interest Driven Sales Funnel is that it's **modular** (plug & play).

This means each Micro Sales Funnel can be plugged in wherever, whenever.

For example, let's say you're launching a new product and you want to build out a Product Launch Micro Sales Funnel. You simply build that funnel, run your audience through it, and end it by returning them to the Main Series where more interests can be identified and more products sold.

This also means it will grow with your business. As you add new products and services to your line with their corresponding Micro Sales Funnels, they plug right into your existing Interest Driven Sales Funnel.

It will grow and expand as you grow and expand.

Ultimately, this makes it incredibly flexible and doesn't bind you in any way.

Timeless Engagement

The Interest Driven Sales Funnel concept is timeless. Meaning, it's not dependent upon a certain piece of technology working a certain way.

I'm doing my best to make the majority of this guidebook timeless so whether you pick it up in 2016, when it's written, or 2026, you'll still glean a tremendous amount of value.

Having said that, in most of the later examples, I'll primarily reference email marketing and automation.

While email marketing is far from dying, it will someday.

The good news is, there will always be a way to reach out and engage your audience:

- Email
- Direct Mail
- Text
- Phone
- Ads & Retargeting
- Visits
- Commercials
- Facebook Messenger
- Whatever method the future holds!

The strategy and concepts you're learning in this guidebook will ring true far into the future.

Entering The Interest Driven Sales Funnel (The Start)

There are many ways an individual can enter an Interest Driven Sales Funnel and a lot is dependent upon how you're engaging your audience.

For example, if you're primarily engaging through email, the person can subscribe to your email list in exchange for a Lead Magnet or after they make a purchase.

Depending on the type of Lead Magnet and/or the product or service they purchased, you may want the individual to go straight into a Micro Sales Funnel where you'll try and sell more.

In other instances, you may want to subscribe the individual directly to the Main Series. For example, if they sign up for a Lead Magnet called,

"How To Start A Blog" – you know they're interested in blogging; however, it's a very complex topic.

Maybe they're only struggling with the technical aspects, or maybe they're not sure how to write content, or they're trying to monetize their blog.

In this instance, use the Main Series to figure out where they're struggling and when they show interest in a particular topic, I'd move them into a Micro Sales Funnel that sells a product or service specific to that issue.

If you're primarily engaging your audience through Facebook Ads, you may run six different ads on six different topics to the same audience. People in your audience will click on the ads that interest them and will then be moved into a Micro Sales Funnel.

Examples

To illustrate the Interest Driven Sales Funnel, here are a couple **timeless** examples.

Old Folks

Let's pretend we sell products that improve the quality of life for old folks.

I'm talking about 75+ years old, living in assisted living communities, where anything that makes their life a tad easier is greatly appreciated.

We can't really email, text, or run ads to these folks because this demographic doesn't typically use computers or cell phones.

So, we'll settle with direct mail and phone calls.

We acquire a list of 10,000 old folks' addresses and begin our Main Series (the left hand, interest gauging side of the diagram on page 5) by sending a postcard about our $100 chair riser (Engagement 1) with the call-to-action (CTA) to give us a call if they want one.

If someone calls, great! They enter into the Micro Sales Funnel that presents several cross-sells.

Our sales rep takes the order for the chair riser, then recommends a $20 E-Z Reacher, a $30 chair attachment to help them stand, and a $150 heated massage pad to ease pain.

After these offers, the customer jumps down to Engagement 4 where we offer our next product.

If the individual doesn't call from Engagement 1, we send a letter with a customer's success story (Engagement 2). It talks about their life before and after the chair riser: how much easier it is to get out of their chair and how their knees feel much better.

The CTA of the letter will again be to give us a call. Of course, our sales rep will take the order and offer the cross-sells of our Micro Sales Funnel.

If the individual doesn't call from Engagement 2, we send a postcard to receive free chair riser blocks (Engagement 3). These free chair riser blocks are nowhere near as good as our $100 chair riser; however, they pique interest and get the individual on the phone, where we can up-sell our nice riser plus all the cross-sells.

If all three engagements for our chair riser fall short, it's no problem. Maybe that person doesn't have trouble getting out of their chair.

They're not interested.

Engagement 4 will recommend another product that solves a completely different problem and so on.

Makes sense, right?

Do you see how it's all pre-planned and thought out?

We send 3 pieces of direct mail about one product that solves a particular problem. If the person calls (shows interest), our sales rep takes them through a pre-established cross-sell series of complementary products we know sell well.

Whether they buy our product or not, they move down to our next offer that solves an entirely different problem.

If they show interest by giving us a call, great! If not, no problem, in another mailing or two, they'll receive an entirely different offer that solves a different problem, and has its own Micro Sales Funnel with up-sells, down-sells, and cross-sells.

McDonalds

McDonalds does a lot of advertising (engaging); however, for this example, I'm only talking about TV ads.

Let's say, for their Main Series, every three months they launch a TV commercial featuring a new product.

The first new product they launch is an ice cream sundae. You don't really like ice cream, so you ignore it. (no interest)

The next product they launch is the McRib!

"Woo!" You say to yourself, "I'm going to McDonalds!" (interest shown)

 You show up at the register, ask for a McRib when they hit you with, "Would you like fries with that?"

Of course you do and a drink to wash it down.

You might as well get the large size, you don't want to be hungry in a few hours.

And, even though you don't really like ice cream, they do have that new sundae; since you're already there, you might as well add it to your order.

Finally, you donate your change to charity.

Before you realize it, instead of spending $4 on a sandwich, you've spent $20 on a meal.

You go back home, feeling nauseous because you shouldn't eat that much McDonalds ever, and wait until another engagement resonates with you.

Closing

Do you now understand why *I see a sales funnel **AS** your business?*

You have different products and services that solve different problems.

You have an audience that consists of many different people with many different interests and many different problems.

The goal, then, is to sync your offerings with your audience in the most efficient and effective way humanly possible.

The best way I know how to do this is with the timeless, but true, Interest Driven Sales Funnel.

The Main Series

Main Series Intro

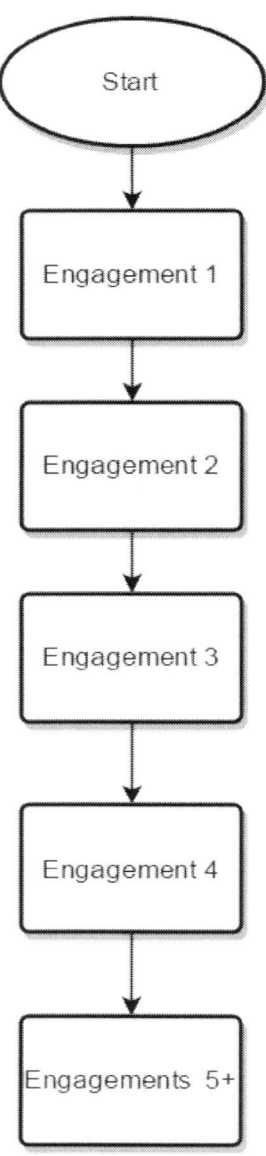

The Main Series is the backbone of your Interest Driven Sales Funnel.

It's responsible for building and maintaining the relationship with your audience while simultaneously **gauging interest**.

Again, the engagements in the Main Series don't necessarily mean emails. Engagements are any form of communication with your audience.

You're simply sending content to see if anyone requests more information.

If someone requests more information (shows interest), they'll enter into a designated Micro Sales Funnel that sells a related product or service, plus the corresponding up-sells, down-sells, and cross-sells.

Pauses, Skips, and Stops

While the Main Series diagram on the left follows a linear path, it may not be exactly one engagement after the other.

For example, if an individual is going through the Main Series and shows interest in a particular product, we may decide to pause the Main Series while they're actively engaged in a Micro Sales Funnel.

In another example, if the individual enters a Micro Sales Funnel and purchases the product or service you're trying to sell, it may make sense to skip down a few engagements to where you're talking about a different product, service, or topic.

Remember, the ultimate goal of the Main Series is to gauge interest. If interest is shown in a particular product, service, or topic – we don't need to get them to show interest in it again and again ... they've already requested more information.

As such, we can pause, skip, and even stop the Main Series, if the audience member has done what we've wanted them to do.

How Many Main Series?

You may be wondering how many Main Series you need for your business.

99% of the time, for a small business, you only need <u>one</u> Main Series.

The only reason you'd ever want more than one Main Series is if you offer products and services to *wildly different* audiences and you have enough offerings to support multiple Main Series.

For example, let's say you own a sports nutrition company that sells supplements and other related goods.

You have two wildly different audiences: bodybuilders and people trying to lose weight.

In this instance, you may want two Main Series because a bodybuilder won't be interested in some crazy diet pill or need motivation to go to the gym. The overweight person won't be interested in the newest bodybuilding supplements or routines.

In this case, by having two Main Series, you won't waste time trying to gauge interest for something they'll never be interested in.

Which Main Series?

Now, if you have more than one Main Series, you may be wondering when, and how, you should assign the individual to a particular one.

You should assign them at the very beginning by *asking them*.

For example, you can offer a 10% off coupon, have a question that asks, "What's your goal: Build Muscle or Lose Weight?", collect their contact information, and add them to the appropriate Main Series.

Another example, I've seen people buy lists of individuals who have previously purchased a diet pill. In this case, it would be fairly safe to assume they're interested in weight loss and can be added to the weight loss Main Series.

Or, You Can Do This …

Creating, developing, and maintaining multiple Main Series is a lot of work.

Unless you have a large enough audience with enough different offerings, it's unlikely viable to have more than one.

Instead, **address both audiences in the same email**.

For example, you can send an email with the first half talking about bodybuilder stuff and the second half talking about weight loss stuff.

Be sure to make the sections obvious so the subscriber can easily tell what pertains to them.

Now, you're killing two birds with one stone!

What About Other Segmentation?

As you probably know, there are a million ways you can dissect your audience based on demographic information, occupation, interests, location, etc.

Continuing with the sports nutrition company example, males and females will likely have very different requirements, as will young vs old.

As such, it can be very beneficial to know this type of information; however, it's not needed for the Main Series.

The Main Series is intended to be general enough to simply gauge interest in a product, service, or topic.

You don't really need to connect on a deeper level at this point.

However, during a Micro Sales Funnel, knowing gender and age may be very beneficial. You can give examples of someone similar to your audience member finding success with a specific product or service.

Main Series Patterns

While you can theoretically "wing" the content and structure of your Main Series because each email (engagement) can stand on its own, it's probably not the best strategy.

It's generally best to follow a pattern or plan for a few reasons:

1) It's more logical for your subscribers and they'll know what to expect
2) It gives your subscribers more chances to show interest in a particular product, service, or topic. Not everyone will act on the first email you send and by presenting your message several times, in several different ways, you give your subscribers more opportunities to act
3) It's easier for you to create content because you know what the content of your next email (engagement) should be

In this section I'll give you several patterns to help you structure your Main Series.

Just remember, the main goal of the Main Series is to gauge interest! This way you are able to send more relevant information to your subscribers and sell more via your Micro Sales Funnels.

The 3 Es

Don't be mad, I know I just made a few points on why you should follow a pattern, but this first "pattern" isn't really a pattern at all.

Instead, it's more a way to think about the emails you send.

Each email you send should have one of these Es as its primary goal:

- **Entertain**: These emails (engagements) are meant to entertain. Videos, pictures, stories, etc. provide great entertainment.

- **Educate**: Helpful emails that solve problems, answer questions, and provide guidance. How-to tutorials, white papers, case studies, etc. provide great educational material.
- **Earn**: These emails drive sales by bringing customers back to your business. Coupons, discounts, bonuses, etc. provide extra incentive to shop.

While each of these emails should have one clear goal or objective (Entertain, Educate, Earn), they don't have to be mutually exclusive.

For example, if you send a how-to video, it should definitely be educational, but why not make it entertaining and offer a CTA to buy something at the end?

When To Use

You may want to use the 3 E emails if you offer TONS of products and services in an incredibly wide variety of categories.

Basically, you should follow this "pattern" when you offer so much "stuff" for a wide variety of interests and you have no idea what the subscriber may be interested in.

For example, if you run a massive ecommerce store (250+ products with 10+ unique product categories) and you have 10 top selling products you really want a new subscriber to see, you may not want to spend a full week promoting each one. It would take 10 weeks for them to see everything you offer.

Instead, you send a daily, 3 E email for 10 consecutive days. This way, the new subscriber will see what you offer much sooner and hopefully show interest in a product or two which will launch them into a Micro Sales Funnel.

How To Use

These emails are very versatile and can stand on their own (the subscriber doesn't need to read the previous email or blog post to understand the email). Each email is its own entity.

If you're sending this type of email, you want to send an email **3-7 times a week**.

The frequency depends on a few factors. The first one being the longevity of the subscriber. For example, a newer subscriber may need more emails initially, especially if you're trying to introduce them to your top 10 selling products.

You also want to take into account how long a typical subscriber stays on your list.

Is the average subscriber on your list for years? Months? Weeks?

How long do you *want* the average subscriber to be on your list?

Are you trying to "churn and burn" them where you're sending an "Earn" email every day for weeks until they unsubscribe? In this case, you can send an email every day for those few weeks.

Or, are you trying to build and maintain a relationship for years to come? In this case, start the first week off with daily emails, but then ease back to maybe 3-4 emails a week. You also want a healthy mix of the 3 Es so you're not just hitting them up for money every day.

The frequency of emails also depends on how you've set expectations. If, when they registered, you said you'd be sending daily emails, then they should receive daily emails. If you said you'd send emails a few times a week, do that.

Closing

Again, these 3 E emails aren't so much a pattern as they are a way to think about what you're sending.

Remember, while each email should have a main objective (entertain, educate, earn), it doesn't mean one email can't do all three!

Weekly "Pushes"

I call this pattern "Weekly Pushes" because every week you're trying to sell (push) a different product or service to your list.

Instead of making random offers and sending random emails depending on your mood, you spend an entire week on the same topic.

This gives people more opportunity to see what you're offering and act, while not being overbearing and "burning" them out.

The Weekly "Pushes" Framework

The goal of this framework is to get the person on the sales page. If the individual views the sales page, we know they're interested in what we have to offer.

Step 1: Pick a widget to sell.

Step 2: Follow the pattern below for that single widget.

- **Pattern**: 3 and 2 (M, T, W, F, S)

Send 4 to 5 emails on the same topic, for the same widget, during each "push". In general, it's good to break up these emails to give people a little time to react, rather than bombarding them every day. For this reason, I recommend sending 3 daily emails, take a day off, send 2 more daily emails, take a day off, and then repeat with a new "push".

- **Email 1**: Fun/personal story

- o Relate to widget
- o PS goes to sales page

People connect with stories. People enjoy stories. We want people to both connect with us and enjoy hearing from us, which is why we must share a story! Now, it doesn't necessarily have to be a personal story; you can share a success story from a client or customer or even a well known individual, like a celebrity, just shared in a different light.

At the end of the story, close out (soft sell) with a simple PS line that takes them to the sales page where they can learn more, if they wish.

- **Email 2**: Promotion of widget
  - o Use a marketing formula: Problem-Agitate-Solve, Feature-Benefits-Advantages, Before-After-Bridge
  - o CTA goes directly to the sales page – "Click Here To Buy"

While stories are great and help us connect, sometimes a good old fashioned sales letter converts best ... especially when they have the story from the previous email rolling around in their head! In this 2nd email, pitch your widget. You can use a marketing formula to help structure your message or do whatever you think is best.

The call-to-action should be straight forward and to the point with no mystery behind it, "If you're interested in this widget, click here". (How much more "interest gauging" can you get?! If the person clicks that link, we know they're interested in our offer and they'll enter one of our Micro Sales Funnels.)

- **Emails 3-4:** Content on topic of widget
  - o Link to a blog post that's entertaining and/or educational
  - o Include CTAs in both the PS line of the email and within the article itself which link to your widget's sales page

After sharing a story and a "hard" pitch, it's time to ease back a little bit and just share some more information with them. Send links to articles, videos, and other resources they'll find helpful, interesting, and entertaining on the same topic as the widget you're trying to sell.

Include links to your widget's sales page in your email PS line and throughout the particular article so they can easily navigate to the sales page, if they're interested in learning more.

- **Email 5**: Content OR Promotion (discount)

Email 5 is optional. If the individual hasn't visited your sales page after 4 emails on the same topic for the same widget ... they may simply not be interested in that offer. So, use some discretion here. If you feel like this 5th email is "too much", don't use it.

If you do use Email 5, you can send another piece of content like emails 3 & 4 OR you can make a last-ditch effort to sell your widget by sending another "hard" sales email and/or by offering a discount.

That completes the Weekly "Pushes" framework! Rinse and repeat with a new product the following week!

Story-Based Series

Story-Based Series are similar to the Weekly "Pushes" in that you're sending more than one email on the same product/service/topic. However, they're different in that all of the emails you send are "connected".

What do I mean by "connected"?

Think about a TV series like Game of Thrones, Orange is the New Black, The Walking Dead, The Sopranos, Breaking Bad ... *hopefully you've watched a TV series before.*

The point is, what do all of these series have in common?

You need to watch all the episodes, in order, to truly enjoy it ... but, once you're "in", you're in and likely end up binge watching the whole series!

How do they suck you in and keep you watching?

Cliffhangers.

Or, as us marketers call them, **opening and closing loops**.

As you're watching a TV series, they introduce five different story lines in one episode, but they don't finish any of them in that episode. Instead, they make you wait until the next episode to see what happens; then, they close two of the previously established story lines ... and start four more!

It's never ending. As soon as one story line ends, two more start – keeping you hooked.

The idea of opening and closing loops is the core concept behind a Story-Based Series.

How To Use It

As I previously stated, send several emails on the same product/service/topic – anywhere from 2 to 10, depending on what you have to share.

As people get sucked into your story and start clicking on links and visiting pages, their actions trigger different Micro Sales Funnels.

Here are a few simple phrases that can be used to open loops:

- More on that later
- You'll find out tomorrow
- In the next email you'll receive X, so be on the lookout for it!

Finally, my last remaining tip is to write all these emails at once. Pick your story, map it out, where are you going to take people, what do you want them to click, how are you going to carry the story across several days. Then, write all 2-10 emails in one go.

These emails can be a rough draft at first, you simply want to make sure you're opening and closing loops in a way that sucks people in.

If you break up how you write your emails, you'll forget which loops you opened and closed and it won't work.

Autoresponder Madness

A fellow by the name of Andre Chaperon is the grandfather of Story-Based Series (he calls them Soap Opera Sequences).

He put together a course called Autoresponder Madness that teaches how to write these Story-Based Series.

It's a solid course and I highly recommend it, if this concept sounds interesting to you!

The course sales page: http://autorespondermadness.com

"Long" Course

The "Long" Course is the pattern I've been using with Crazy Eye Marketing for about a year.

Think of it as if you're teaching your subscriber something long and complex. Consider every email (engagement) you send a lesson.

In my case, I teach the sales funnel concept by taking people through the sections they need to focus on, based on their order of importance and significance.

Of course, along the way, I dribble in different products and services I offer that make sales funnel development easier for my subscribers.

When To Use It

The "Long" Course model won't fit every type of business; however, it works very well for businesses that offer courses/training/coaching and other services. You teach through this series and it makes a natural transition into selling a course, training, or coaching.

You also want to be able to provide a "linear" path for success - there's a Point A and a Point B with clear steps to successfully get from Point A to Point B.

Back to my sales funnel "Long" Course example, the path for all sales funnels is the same: customers, business, delivery, the "meat", emails, traffic, etc.

It's a logical path to get from Point A to Point B.

Another example, weight loss: mindset, diets (simple to complex), exercising (walk, run, first 5k), supplements, etc.

This is another linear path from Point A to Point B. Of course, many people who are trying to lose weight jump straight to supplements and diet pills; however, the right way is to follow the "Long" course described above.

Example

I think the best way to describe the "Long" Course pattern is by providing an example. Picture it like this:

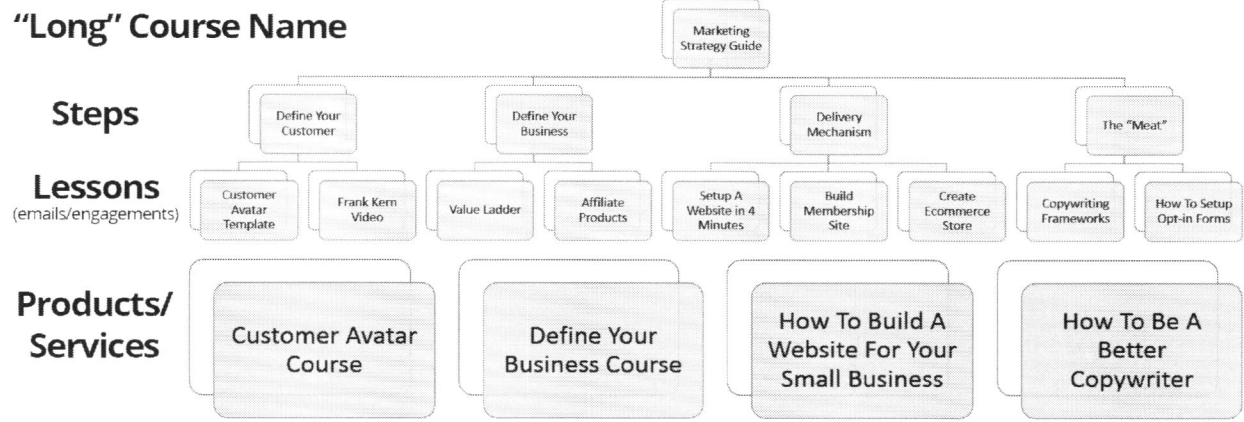

- **"Long" Course Name**: You should give it a name!
- **Steps**: How to get from Point A to Point B
- **Lessons (emails/engagements)**: The particular blog posts, videos, podcasts, etc. you will send to your subscribers to teach them something about the particular step they're on
- **Products/Services**: The corresponding products/service you offer as they relate to each step and/or lesson

As you can see, the "Long" Course is simply your content (blog posts, videos, white papers, reports, etc.) presented in an order that takes an individual from Point A to Point B.

Again, if you offer courses, training, coaching, or services – this pattern can be very effective!

Combining Patterns

I briefly want to address the fact the aforementioned Main Series patterns can certainly be combined.

For example, the majority of my Main Series for Crazy Eye Marketing is a long course. It works very well for what I offer and the market I serve. However, there are segments of it that are more 3 E styled and other segments that are Weekly "Pushes".

Remember, **the point of the Main Series is to gauge interest** while building and maintaining a relationship.

You know your audience better than anyone else, if you think one pattern will work for one product and another pattern for another – mix it up! Or, better yet, split test to see which pattern performs better!

Micro Sales Funnels

Micro Sales Funnels

We've made it to the section you're probably most excited about – the Micro Sales Funnels!

These are the "typical" sales funnels you probably envision when you think of and read about sales funnels.

They're the up-sell funnels, webinar funnels, product launch funnels, book funnels, call back funnels, and any other type of funnel you can think of.

Of course, every "guru" has their own take and twist on how these things can, and should, function; however, their goal remains the same – **to sell something.**

Now, let's talk about these awesome funnels and how to use them!

Quick Overview

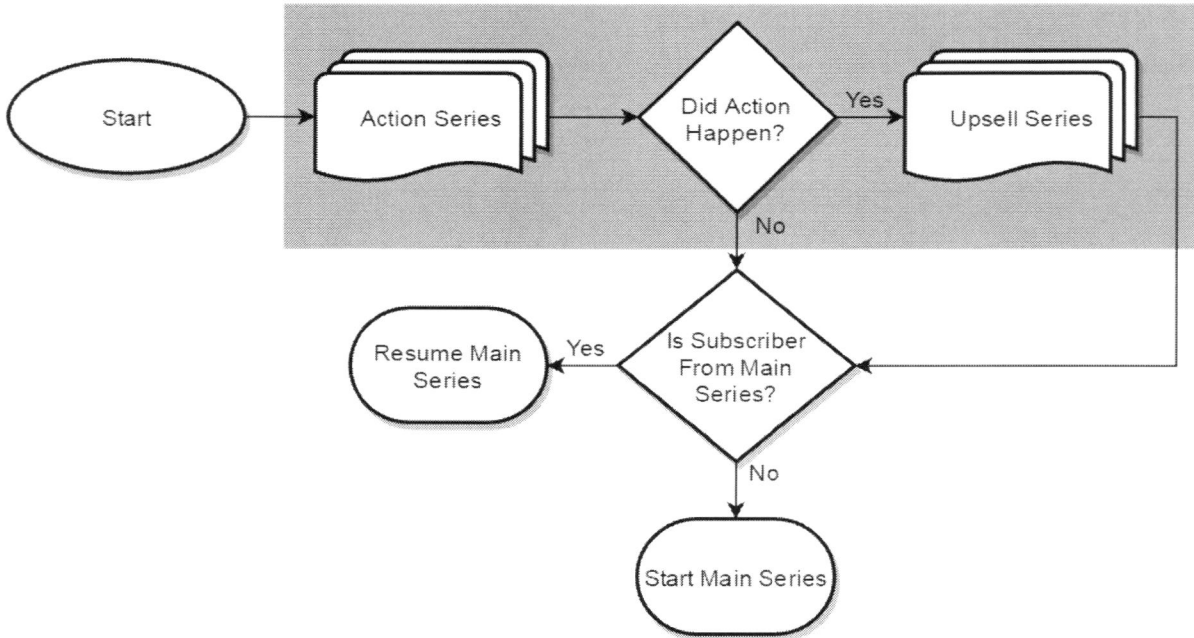

Above is an example of what a Micro Sales Funnel can look like.

No matter what the middle section contains, the Start and End will look the same.

The Start

The Start occurs when an individual shows interest.

But, what exactly does that mean?

Interest can be shown in a variety of ways:

- **Click** – Someone clicks a link in one of your emails showing they're interested in a certain topic, product, service, etc.
- **Pageview** – When someone looks at a specific page on your website, it shows they're interested in a certain topic, product, service, etc.
- **Purchase** – When an individual purchases a product or service from you, it's a dead giveaway they're interested in a certain topic, product, service, etc.
- **Specific Lead Magnet** – When someone opts-in to receive a Lead magnet for something related to what you want to sell. For example, a mini-guide called "5 ways we decreased Facebook Ad spending by 89%" – we know they're interested in Facebook Ads.
  - o *Note:* In Annex A you will find a Specific Lead Magnet plan that will blow your mind!
- **Phone Call / Reply** – If someone calls or replies to one of your emails, depending on the reasoning behind it, it could certainly show interest in a particular product, service, topic, etc.
- **Survey** – Similar to a phone call or reply in that someone is explicitly telling you what they're interested in.
- **Points (CRM)** – More "advanced"; however, if you're using a CRM tool you can use points to gauge interest and trigger Product/Service Sales Funnels based on points. For example, if someone looks at your sales page 5 times, you know they're

highly interested and may just need a tad more persuasion - exactly what a Micro Sales Funnel will provide.

As you can see, there are many ways an individual can enter one of your Micro Sales Funnels.

After The Start (The Funnel Part)

After the Start, you have the "funnel part." Again, this can look like pretty much anything; however, in the example above we use an Action Series and an Upsell Series.

- **Action Series** – An email series that addresses the subscriber from different angles in order to try to "connect" with them and drive them to take action (make a purchase). For example, one email could be very logical and explain, by-the-numbers, why your deal is great. The next email could be a story about someone who found success with your product. Another email could be benefits driven and explain the results one can expect.

- **Upsell Series** – A series of emails triggered by an action (purchase) and attempts to move them to the next logical step. For example, they purchase a $7 guide to solve a problem and the upsell is a step-by-step video course for $97.

The End

Just like the Start, the End will be the same no matter what the "funnel part" looks like.

If the individual entered into your Micro Sales Funnel from your Main Series – they will re-enter the Main Series and pick up right where they left.

If the individual entered into your Product/Service Sales Funnel via another source, ie. Facebook Ad to a Specific Lead Magnet or they made a direct purchase, they'll start the Main Series from the top.

The "Simplest" Sales Funnel

This first Micro Sales Funnel model is even more basic than the example I outlined above; however, don't let its simplicity fool you – *there's beauty in simplicity*.

As with all Micro Sales Funnels, the Start is when interest is shown.

After an interest is shown, an Action Series is triggered. While I'll go into greater detail on Action Series later in this guidebook, for the time being – **an Action Series is a series of emails (engagements) that try and motivate the audience member to take action (ie. buy something).**

Whether the individual performs the action we want them to or not, the funnel will end just like any other Micro Sales Funnel. The individual will either be returned to their previous location within the Main Series or, in the instance of a new subscriber, they will start at the beginning of the Main Series.

If the idea of adding any of the next few Micro Sales Funnel models sounds too daunting, try adding a few of "Simplest" Sales Funnels and you'll start to see some amazing things happen!

For example, one of my students added seven of these funnels to his pre-established Main Series and here are his results:

	Open Rate	CTR	EPC	% Improvement		
				Open Rate	CTR	EPC
Main Series	15.26%	3.58%	$ 0.01			
AS 1	49.01%	26.23%	$ 1.33	221.17%	632.68%	13200.00%
AS 2	48.48%	25.30%	$ 2.22	217.69%	606.70%	22100.00%
AS 3	44.74%	24.73%	$ 1.90	193.18%	590.78%	18900.00%
AS 4	54.83%	19.15%	$ 0.35	259.31%	434.92%	3400.00%
AS 5	36.93%	19.12%	$ 0.50	142.01%	434.08%	4900.00%
AS 6	26.93%	6.10%	$ 5.87	76.47%	70.39%	58600.00%
AS 7	34.48%	6.02%	$ 0.13	125.95%	68.16%	1200.00%

The average open rate for his Main Series was 15.26%, Click-Through-Rate (CTR) was 3.58%, and Earnings-Per-Click (EPC) was $0.01.

While the open rate is a little low and he probably needs to address his subject lines, his emails have an above average CTR. This shows he's able to gauge interest based on what links people are clicking.

Also, the EPC for his Main Series was only $0.01, which is perfectly fine. Remember, the intent of the Main Series is to gauge interest while continuing to build and maintain relationships.

The AS # represents the individual Action Series. In this case, each Action Series was triggered after an individual looked at one of his products' sales pages. Each Action Series contained only three emails and most of the content was third party product reviews with a call-to-action (CTA) to visit the sales page and buy the product now!

Very simple.

However, as you can see, every Action Series outperformed the Main Series in open rate, CTR, and EPC by a landslide!

Again, all he did was add the "Simplest" Sales Funnels (Action Series).

He didn't incorporate any up-sells or cross-sales. He kept everything really simple; however, his results have been tremendous!

Conclusion

The "Simplest" Sales Funnel is the starting point. This should be your first journey into the wild and crazy world of Micro Sales Funnels.

The good news is while they're really easy to setup, they can make a massive impact to your bottom line!

The "Classic" Sales Funnel

The next Micro Sales Funnel is certainly the most popular and infamous ; McDonalds built their empire based on it.

"Would you like fries with that?"

Yes, I'm talking about the "Classic" up-sell funnel.

This type of funnel is the true money maker because it directly increases customer order size, and thus, lifetime value.

Understand This...

I'm about to throw several different diagrams at you all named "Classic" Sales Funnels.

It may be overwhelming, especially if you've not seen something like this before.

Ultimately, I want you to understand the premise of the "Classic" Sales Funnel. If someone buys something, you try to sell them more. If they don't buy it, you offer a down-sell or follow up and attempt to make the sale later.

No matter which of the fancy "Classic" Sales Funnel diagrams you're looking at, remember - if your customer purchases something, sell more. If not, down-sell or follow up to sell later.

How To View This Type Of Funnel

Before getting into the fancy diagrams, I need to clarify how to view these "Classic" Sales Funnels as they can quickly become complex.

There are two perspectives to take into consideration when designing your "Classic" Sales Funnels:

- Long-term: Emails or engagements between offers
- Instant: Order flow (at checkout)

Due to these two different perspectives, these funnels can look very different depending on your business model, what you're trying to accomplish, and your platform.

It doesn't always make sense to include emails or other engagements between offers.

Maybe what you *really* want to sell is *after* the individual goes through this funnel.

For example, coaches will frequently use a "Classic" Sales Funnel to sell digital courses and training, in order to get people in the door. But, what they *really* want to sell is private coaching. Instead of really focusing on getting people through the "Classic" Sales Funnel, they just keep it really simple and place all their focus on a Product Launch Funnel, Webinar Funnel, or Call / Application Funnel.

Finally, in other instances, you may be limited by your particular platform and want to consider adding a 3rd party tool like ClickFunnels.

The "Classic" Sales Funnel Models

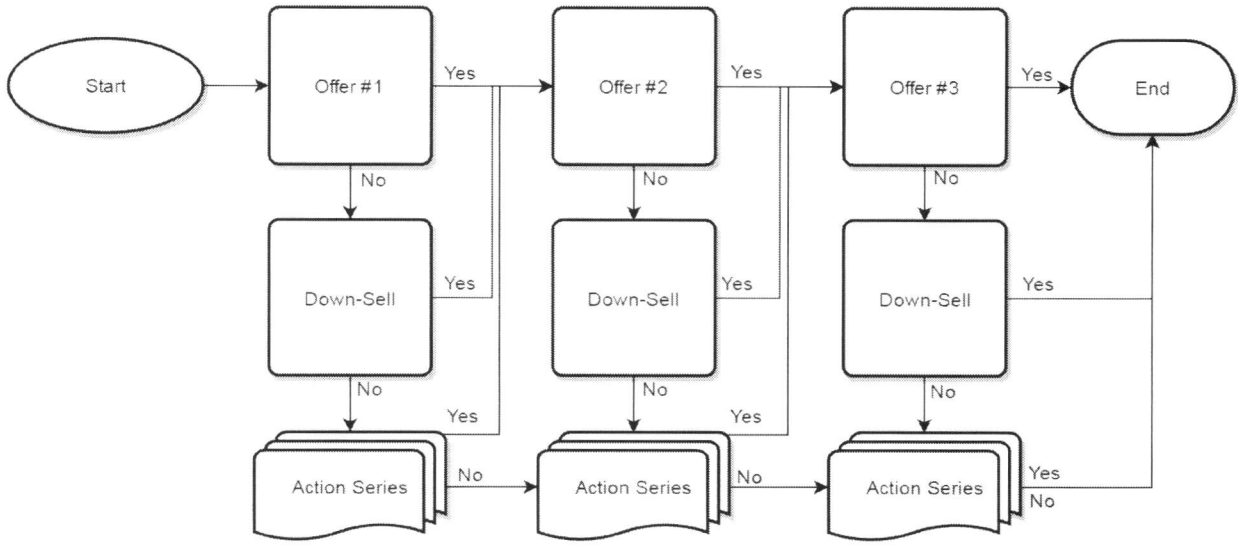

I call this first one the "Mega Classic" Sales Funnel because it's about as complex as "Classic" Sales Funnels can get.

Basically, the big idea is this:

If someone buys something, you make another offer right away (at checkout). If they buy it, you make another offer; however, if they don't buy it, you either down-sell or send emails (engagements).

9 times out of 10, your funnels will not be this complex. There are a lot of moving parts, which means it can break easily. A broken funnel isn't going to do you any good.

However, I wanted to open your eyes to what is possible.

Conversely, this is also a "Classic" Sales Funnel:

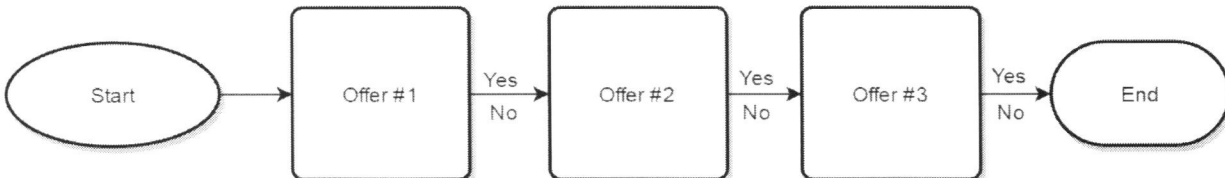

Very simple.

This version would likely occur at checkout and can be considered an order flow.

Basically, the big idea is this:

Regardless of whether someone buys the previous product, you're going to make more offers. There won't be any down-sells or follow up on previous offers – it's either a yes or no on the spot, and that's it.

This is essentially the McDonald's funnel – the funnel starts when you purchase a burger, then they offer fries, then a drink, then to supersize it, then a sundae, and finally to opportunity to donate to a charity. Before you know it, you've spent $20 on a $1 burger!

More often than not, you'll use a version between the "Mega Classic" and the simple funnel above.

One version that's really popular in the Internet marketing world is the **"Trip Wire Funnel"**.

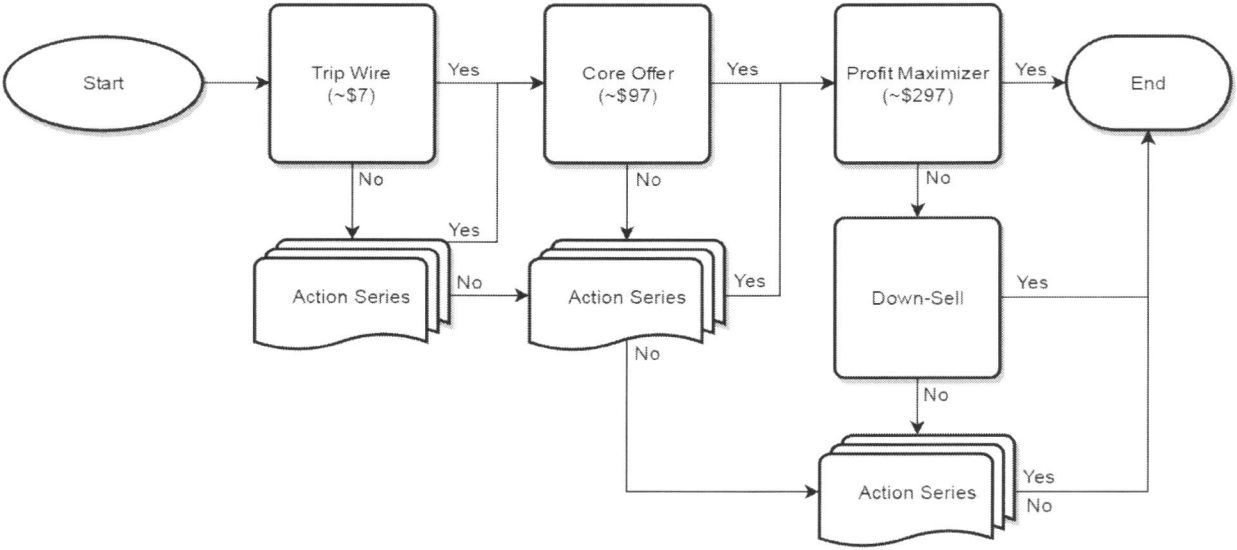

The theory behind this funnel is that as soon as you get someone to open their wallet and spend some money with you, they're much more likely to continue spending.

It starts with offering a low priced product that's too good to pass up called a "trip wire". People buy this product like it's going out of style and "trip" into your funnel where you sell your "Core Product" (what you really want to sell) and your "Profit Maximizer" (a high-end product or service that really rings the cash register).

A frequently seen trip wire is a free + shipping offer for a book. This works incredibly well because a physical book has a relatively high perceived value and opens the door to sell courses and coaching. *This book is one of my trip wires ;)*

If you have a great complementary offer for the front-end, the "Classic" Sales Funnel model below may work well for you:

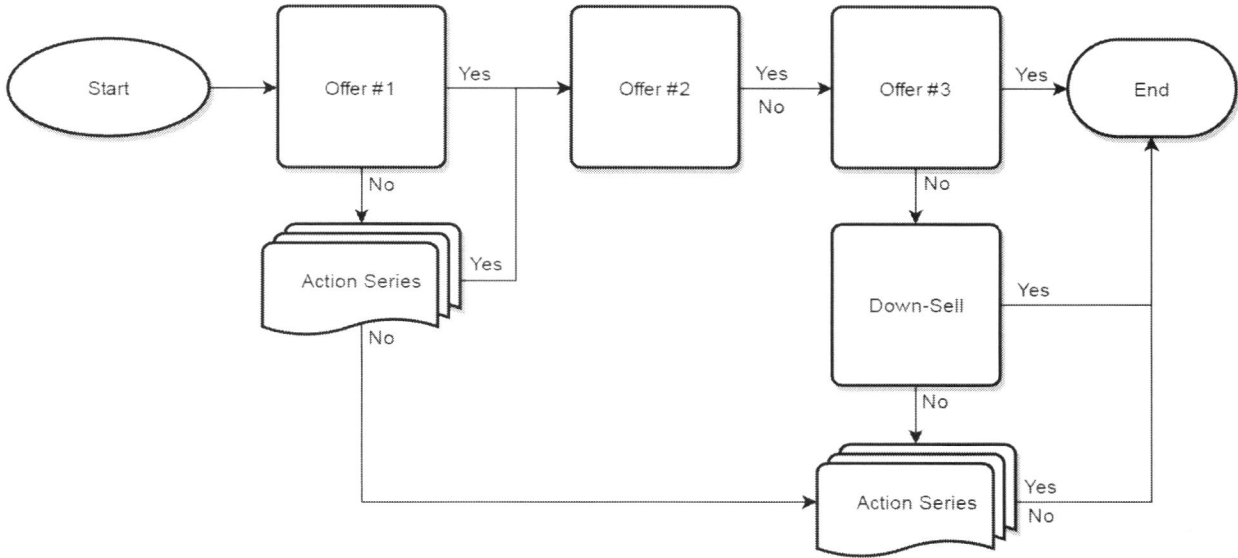

Basically, you work hard to sell your front-end offer (Offer #1) so they see Offer #2. Offer #2 is a complementary product to Offer #1, meaning it's only really helpful if they've purchased Offer #1. Offer #3 is generally a stand-alone offer, meaning you don't need Offer #1 or Offer #2 for it to be great, and it's usually higher priced.

If they don't purchase Offer #3 right away, they'll be offered a down-sell and finally an Action Series in a last-ditch effort to make the sale.

Conclusion

The "Classic" Sales Funnel is the most popular Micro Sales Funnel because it works very well and can make a dramatic impact on the bottom line.

While the "Classic" Sales Funnel can look very different depending upon your unique setup, its purpose remains the same – **to sell more**. This, of course, can be accomplished across a wide timeframe through emails and other engagements and/or instantaneously at checkout.

The Product Launch Funnel

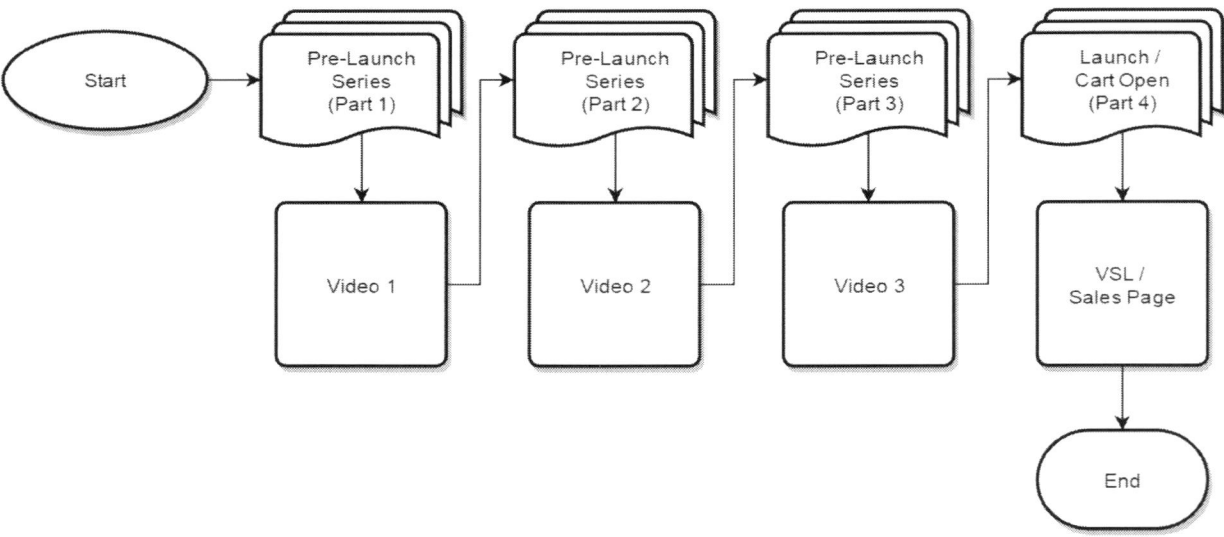

The Product Launch Funnel is wildly popular for more expensive products, like digital courses.

It's typically three content based videos, that entertain and educate, and concludes with a fourth video that makes the offer.

The general flow is this:

Someone shows interest in your upcoming product launch by opting-in, clicking a link, viewing a page, etc. – all the normal "interest gauging" triggers.

From there, they receive a few emails (engagements) directing them to video 1. After they watch the first video, they receive emails about video 2. They watch it, and then receive emails about video 3. They watch it and then receive emails to video 4, which is typically a Video Sales Letter (VSL).

The power behind this funnel comes from two key aspects:

First, this funnel provides insane value in videos 1-3 by giving away your "best stuff". If you do these videos right, it will make your offer a no-brainer. People will think, "If his free stuff is this amazing ... I can't imagine how *absolutely incredible* his paid stuff is!"

The second source of this funnel's power comes from the Launch / Cart Open phase.

During this phase scarcity is introduced because **the cart will close**.

There are a few ways to close the cart. The way you do it depends on whether your Product Launch Funnel is a true, one-time event or if it's evergreen (always available).

If it's a true, one-time event, then it's easy to introduce scarcity because you're going to take the offer off the table at a certain date and time. If the individual misses it, too bad.

If it's an evergreen launch, you need to introduce scarcity in another manner because you won't be removing the offer. You can do this by removing bonuses or by increasing the price, if they don't purchase by a certain date.

The Video Pattern

Before I go any further, I want to address something – I keep saying "video"; however, you don't necessarily need videos. You could use other resources like blog posts or PDFs to develop a product launch series.

Videos are often used because digital video courses are typically sold during a product launch funnel. It makes sense to keep everything in the same medium.

With that being said, you should follow a pattern or strategy for delivering the first three videos. There's some psychology and positioning at play.

There's a proven science behind this content and there are folks that make millions regularly from these product launch funnels.

While I'll give you my particular formula in a moment, I want to share two other guys' formulas … or at least where to get them. (It wouldn't be ethical, and it's probably illegal, to just paste their formulas here; however, you can get them straight from the books I'm about to recommend. Each book is less than $10, but contains invaluable information.)

- Jeff Walker's *"Launch"*: http://www.thelaunchbook.com/
  - Pages 89-97
- Russel Brunson's *"DotCom Secrets"*: https://dotcomsecretsbook.com/
  - Pages 222-227

My Formula: Teach, To-Do, & Tease

While I typically follow the aforementioned formulas because they know what they're doing, I sometimes find them hard to follow. They require certain information to be presented, like success stories.

Success stories are important, and you need to have people find success with your product; however, there's a chicken and egg situation here. You can't really have success stories (besides your own) before your product exists, right?

While you can do a limited pre-launch to get feedback and success stories, doing so takes time and requires an audience.

If you're short on time and/ir lack an audience, what I'm about to explain may work very well for you!

I call it the "Teach, To-Do, & Tease" formula. In each video, you teach something, give the individual a simple task, and tease what's to come.

I'll explain this formula through an example.

Let's pretend I'm selling an expensive course titled, "How to Become a World-Class Facebook Ads Guru".

Across the Product Launch Funnel, I would teach a segment of the course.

Which segment? Either the "coolest" part or the beginning. Sometimes you can't teach the "coolest" part because your course is progressive and you can't do the "cool" stuff without having completed steps 1-5 first.

You also want to ensure the segment you teach **provides a clear deliverable**.

Think of it like a mini-course with a beginning, middle, and end.

Basically, whether or not they purchase the full course, I want them to receive at least one clear result from my training.

You never want to leave anyone feeling like they've been duped ... like you've just dragged them along so you could sell them your product.

You want them to accomplish *something*, and if they want more – there's a full course on the topic.

Back to the example, regarding Facebook Ads, I can't start with the "cool" stuff because without having the proper groundwork in place, the "cool" stuff can't happen.

The segment taught is the beginning and it's titled, "How to build custom audiences that know, like, and trust you with Facebook's advertising platform."

In video 1, I'll teach people how to install the Facebook tracking pixel on their website, tell them to go do it, and tease the conversion tracking training coming in video 2.

In video 2, I'll teach them how to track conversions and create custom conversions which will help them create specific audiences ... which is what is covered in video 3.

In video 3, I'll teach them how to create custom audiences based on pages viewed, conversions made, and how to use this to create lookalike audiences of similar people that will know, like, and trust you!

Finally, in video 4, I'll pitch the full course by explaining what they just learned will help them tremendously moving forward; however, it's only a small segment of becoming a World-Class Facebook Ads Guru!

See how it's all a natural flow into selling the full product? It doesn't require having testimonials and success stories because you're helping them find success!

If you help someone solve a problem for free, they're more likely to reciprocate when you're trying to solve a bigger problem for money.

Conclusion

The Product Launch Funnel works great when selling high priced products, like digital courses, because it gives you the opportunity to "prove" yourself before asking for the sale.

You also want to follow a proven pattern for your videos because there is psychology and reasoning behind the content of each one.

Finally, you need to open and close the cart and make it a big deal by introducing some form of scarcity.

The Webinar Funnel

In the good ol' days, people and businesses used to host seminars, but now they can get in front of more people faster and more easily via webinars.

These types of sales funnels have become wildly popular recently due to the fact they convert like gangbusters!

Here's a common Webinar Sales Funnel:

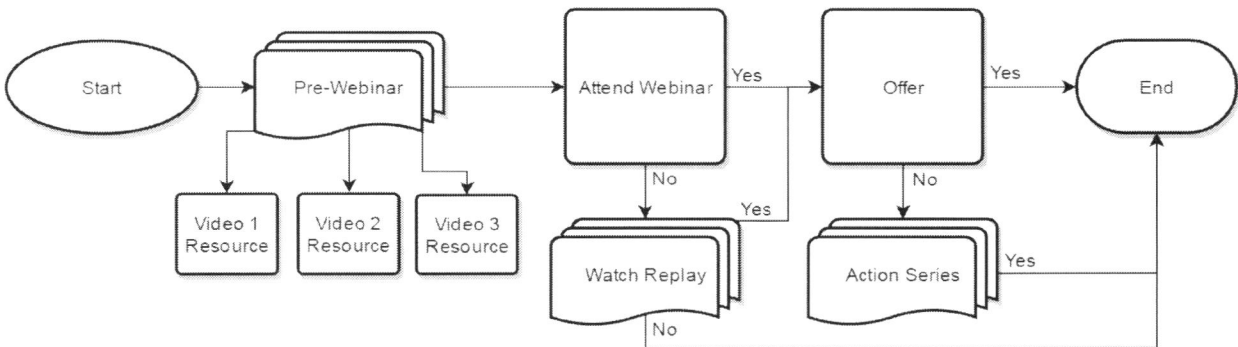

Similar to the Product Launch Funnel, the Webinar Funnel is typically used for higher-priced products and services because you have people with you for 60+ minutes. This gives you enough time to convey your message fully, give the pitch, and answer questions.

While you can automate your webinar to make it evergreen, the live aspect gives these presentations their power.

When it's live, everything comes across as fresh, new, and when you give your call-to-action, there's an inherent sense of urgency. You're ending the presentation at X time, and once it's over, the deal is gone.

The general flow is this:

Someone shows interest in your webinar by opting-in via a webinar registration page. They're then enrolled in your pre-webinar autoresponder series where you send a few videos and resources to prime and excite the individual for the upcoming webinar. Then, you host your webinar.

Ideally, the individual attends your webinar, sees your offer, purchases it, and ends the Micro Sales Funnel.

But, if they don't attend your webinar, you can send a "replay autoresponder series" which consists of a few emails that present the individual the opportunity to watch a replay of the webinar.

Hopefully they watch the replay, see your offer, purchase it, and end the Micro Sales Funnel.

If they don't watch the webinar or the replay, they won't see the offer, so this particular Micro Sales Funnel is ended.

If the individual sees the offer, either during the live webinar or the replay, but doesn't purchase it, you can follow up with an Action Series. The Action Series tries to sell them on it by answering more questions, handling objections, sharing more success stories, or even offering a discount in a last-ditch effort to make the sale.

Turning It Evergreen

While the great power of webinars comes from being live, you can still create the same live feel and automate the entire process.

By turning your webinar into an evergreen presentation, you're able to give presentations 24/7/365!

There are a million different tools to help you do this; however, there are two elements a tool can't provide that you must take into account before going the evergreen route.

First, the webinar you turn evergreen **needs to be a recorded live webinar**.

This means you can't sit in your office, record yourself talking about some slides, editing the clip to cut out the "uhs", and then launch your evergreen webinar.

Remember, the power of webinars comes from being *live*. People can tell in a heartbeat if something was scripted and performed alone or held live.

If someone attends your webinar and they're presented with a scripted presentation, it will come across as unauthentic.

Don't get me wrong, scripted, pre-recorded, and edited presentations are fine; however, call it a presentation or training – don't call it a webinar.

A webinar has the connotation of being live and if you don't fulfil that, people aren't going to be as happy and excited.

Plus, there are benefits of performing live. You see what does and doesn't work, what questions people have, etc. – it really helps to refine your presentation.

The strategy, then, is to hold a handful of live webinars, get some real time feedback, adjust your presentation, then record one and use it as your evergreen webinar.

The second element you need to provide is **a way to contact you**, the presenter. This can be something as simple as a chat box below the webinar.

As much as humanly possible, no matter if the webinar itself is pre-recorded, you want to be live in the chat room to field any questions.

Some people are ready to buy; however, they will have the simplest question stopping them from whipping out their credit card. If you're able to answer their question immediately – you'll get yourself a new customer!

Live chat may not always be possible, especially if you're running webinars 24/7/365, so the second best option is to follow up via email; however, you lose the "in the moment" momentum, which may result in lost sales.

Either way, you need to make yourself present as much as possible, even if the webinar itself is recorded.

Other Webinar Blueprints

Just like with the "Classic" Sales Funnel, there are a bunch of ways to layout a Webinar Sales Funnel depending on your needs.

There are arguments for and against offering replays and follow up emails that pitch the offer.

Some webinars are live, four hour long events and only during those four hours can you purchase the offer.

While others are heavy on getting individuals to watch the replay and follow up intensely on the offer.

No one way works better than the other all the time, just figure out what works best for you!

Self-Liquidating Offer

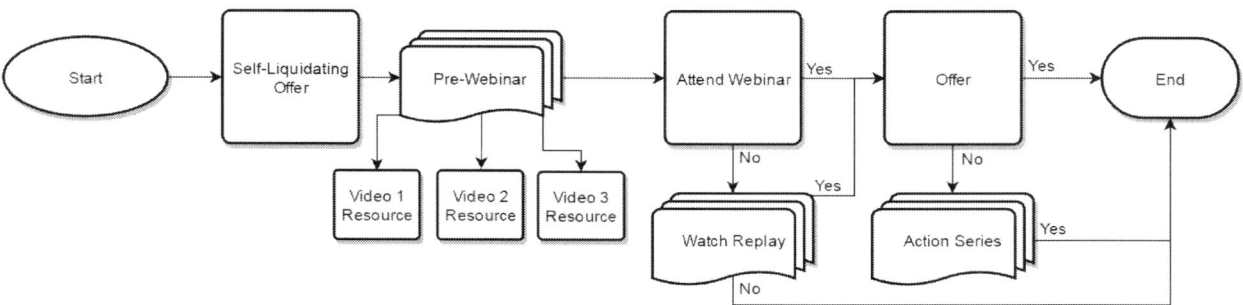

This blueprint looks similar to the original with one exception, immediately after registering for the webinar, the individual is met with a Self-Liquidating Offer or SLO.

A SLO is similar to a Trip Wire, in fact, their names are often used interchangeably. It's typically priced under $10 and is too good to refuse; however, a SLO doesn't necessarily "trip" someone into the other offers.

Instead, its sole purpose is to recoup ad spend to acquire leads.

Offer Up!

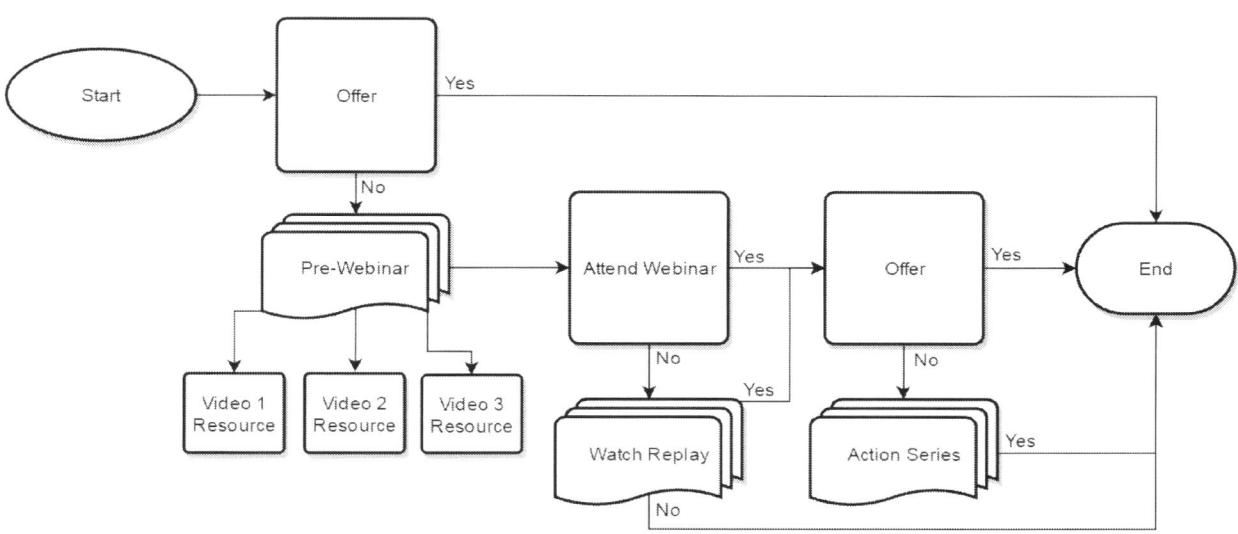

This blueprint is similar to the SLO example above in that the subscriber is immediately greeted with an offer upon registering for the webinar; however, in this instance they're met with the *main* offer.

There are a couple reasons you may want to try this:

In some instances, people will buy your offer right away without going through the entire webinar process. They get what they want faster and you don't have to work as hard!

Another theory is that by seeing the offer first, they're primed for when you make your official pitch. They say it takes 6-8 touches before you'll make the sale, this is a simple way to add another touch.

No Pre-Webinar

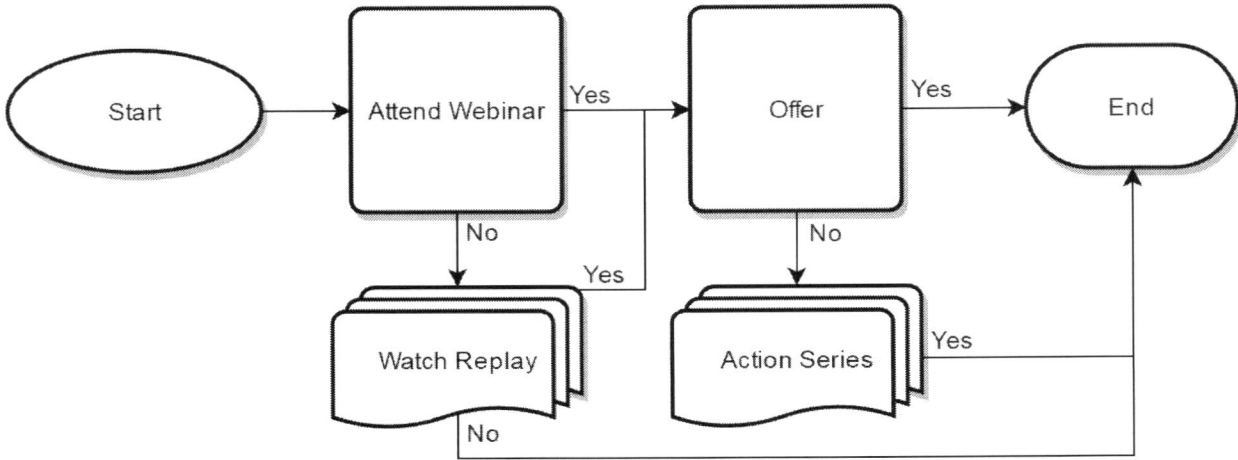

In many instances, especially if your webinar is evergreen, you won't have enough time to go through an entire pre-webinar series … and you don't have to!

No Pre-Webinar, No Replay

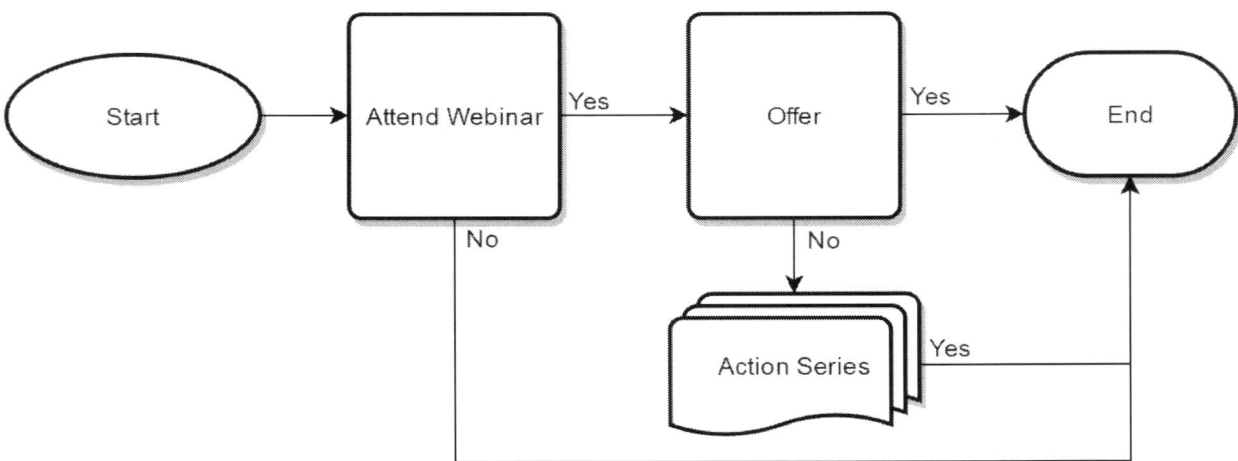

If you don't want to offer a replay, don't!

The Webinar Presentation

Just like with the Product Launch Funnel, there's an art and science behind the content you present in your webinar.

Before you launch your own webinar, make sure you attend a bunch of webinars – especially those in the same niche as you **that you know are successful**.

Since launching a webinar is a piece of cake, every small business on the planet has one. Unfortunately, not all are successful and you don't want to emulate those.

Attend the successful ones. Take notes on how they open, present their content, and pitch their offer.

Understand how they engage with their audience and handle objections.

Pay attention and really study what they do. It's going to help you tremendously.

Finally, I recommend grabbing Russel Brunson's Perfect Webinar training from https://perfectwebinarsecrets.com/.

It costs less than $5 and contains about three hours of training. He outlines, step-by-step, how to structure your webinar presentation for maximum effectiveness.

Conclusion

The Webinar Sales Funnel is an effective way to sell higher end products and services. They give you enough time to go into detail on your offer plus the live aspect makes them really engaging.

Having the ability to answer questions and squash objections on the spot makes them incredibly powerful.

There's also the opportunity to make them evergreen so they're working for your 24/7/365. But, when you turn a webinar evergreen, make sure it's a recorded live version and you make yourself available to answer questions.

Finally, before launching your own webinar, make sure you study other successful webinars to really get a good grasp on how to present yours.

The Call / Application Sales Funnel

While Product Launch and Webinar Funnels are great for selling many types of high-ticket products and services, sometimes you really need to talk to the individual before they feel comfortable making the purchase.

Other times, you need to feel comfortable selling them the product or service. You may want to qualify them before moving forward on a deal.

Naturally, these situations typically entail talking to the potential customer/client, which is why we have the Call / Application Sales Funnel:

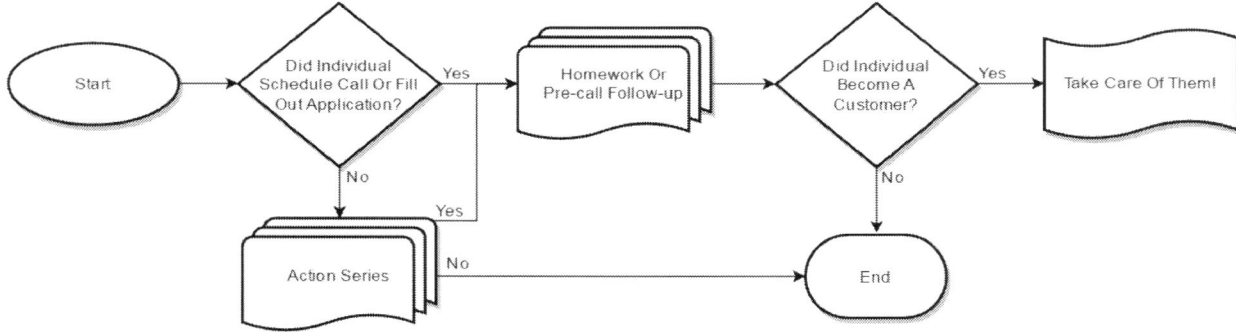

The general flow is this:

An individual starts the funnel by clicking a "contact" or "application" link in an email or on your site. Or, they may opt-in to contact you (2-step, more on it later).

From there, the individual either schedules a call with you or fills out your application. Or they don't.

Assuming they do, they receive the "Homework Or Pre-call Follow-up" autoresponder series.

- **Homework**: Works as both a qualifier and as a chance to sell yourself more. The homework is typically something simple, like watching a few videos so they are prepared for the upcoming call.

   If they do the homework, great! You know they're highly interested. If not, then maybe they're not the right customer for you.

- **Pre-call Follow-up**: This follow-up series can be used similarly to the "Homework" setup outlined above in that you give some material to consume. It also serves to remind the individual they have an upcoming call with you.

   People will forget they've scheduled a call with you. Fortunately, most scheduling tools have built-in functionality for sending reminder emails. You can set it up to send a call reminder 24 hours, 4 hours, and 20 minutes out.

Hopefully, the individual does the homework and/or you speak to them and they become a customer of yours. Now all you have to do is serve them!

If they don't become a customer, they end this Micro Sales Funnel and either enter or resume the Main Series so you can begin gauging more interests.

Let's go back to the beginning of this Micro Sales Funnel – "Did Individual Schedule Call Or Fill Out Application?"

A lot of people will land on your call scheduling and/or application forms without actually filling them out.

You don't want to ignore these people because they've shown interest in your offer.

In this case, follow up via an Action Series with the CTA being to schedule the call or fill out the application.

Hopefully, they do what you want and will flow through the rest of the Micro Sales Funnel; however, if they don't, they either enter or resume the Main Series.

The 2-Step Approach

While you're able to easily track people's actions and gauge their interests when they're already on your list – you don't want to miss out on people that aren't on your list.

To capture these new people, I recommend the 2-Step Approach.

It works like this - before an individual even lands on your call scheduling or application form, they enter their email address.

For example:

An individual clicks on the "Schedule A Call" button in the top navigation menu:

Clicking that button pops up a lightbox opt-in form that requests their email address:

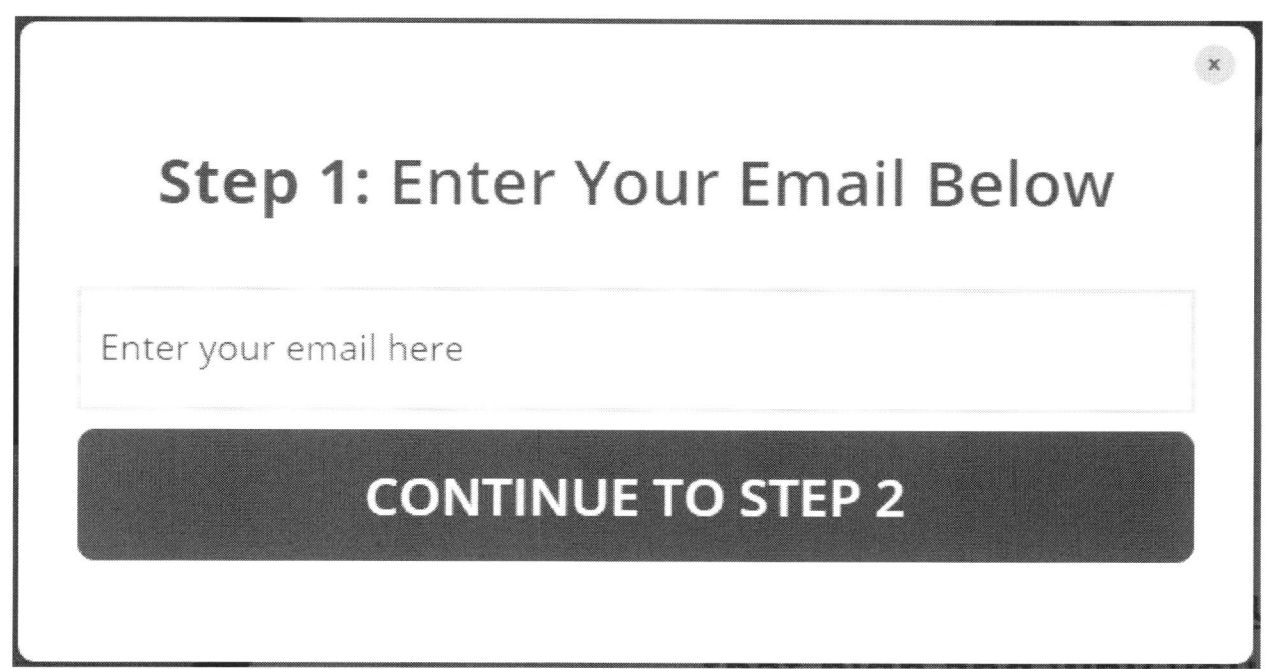

It makes perfect sense these steps would be required to schedule a call - ie. "Step 1: Enter Your Email Below" and "Continue To Step 2".

Step 2 is simply the scheduling or application form:

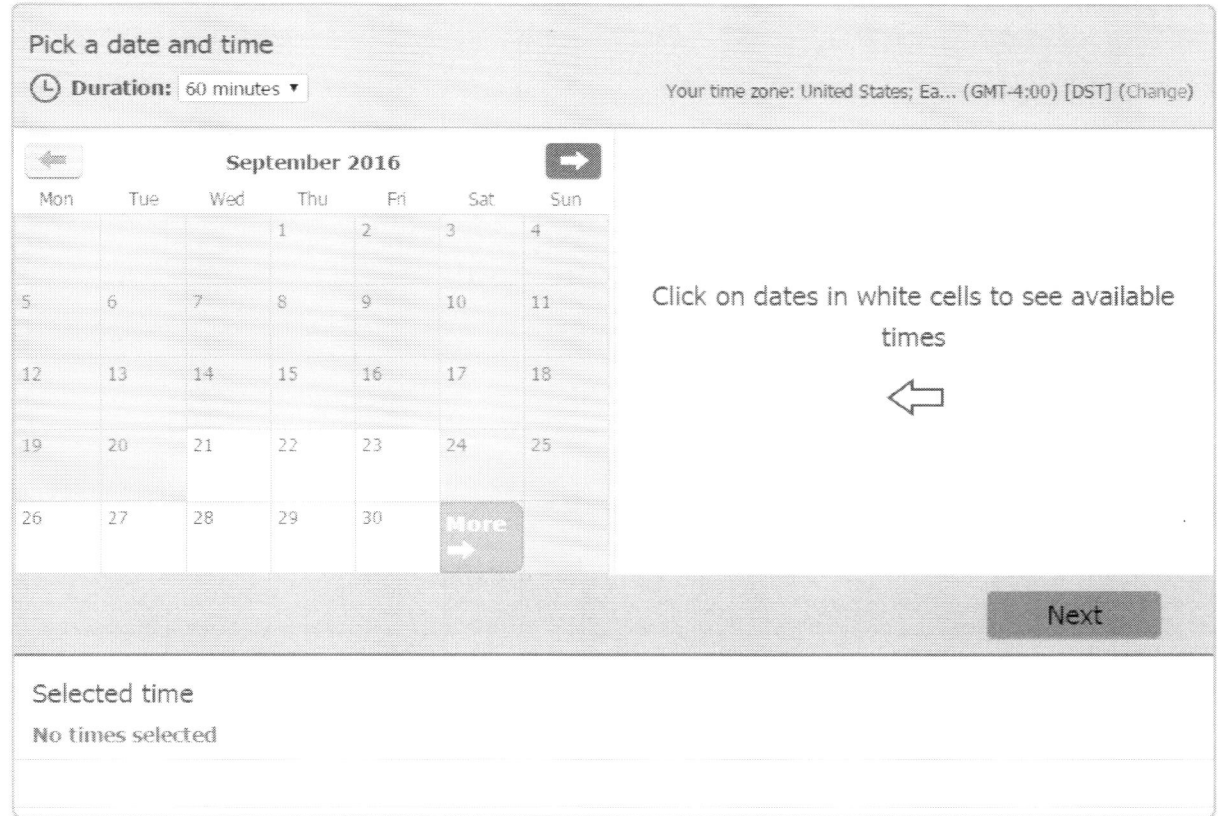

Again, hopefully they go straight through the process; however, if they don't – you collected their email address in "Step 1", and are able to follow up with an Action Series that motivates them to finish the process.

Conclusion

The Call / Application Funnel is perfect for when you need to talk to someone or need them to fill out an application to prove they are a good fit.

If you offer personalized services, this funnel might be one to check out and implement!

Other Funnels

As I stated at the beginning of this section, every sales funnel "guru" has their own sales funnel model(s) they teach.

This is great! More people to learn from and more models to follow and implement.

Even greater, they all work with the Interest Driven Sales Funnel concept – they're all [typically] Micro Sales Funnels.

You still incorporate your interest gauging Main Series and when an interest in a product or service is shown, instead of launching one of the Micro Sales Funnels outlined above, you simply launch that particular "guru's" funnel.

After the individual has gone through that funnel, they hop back into the Main Series and continue their journey until they show interest in something else.

The Interest Driven Sales Funnel concept is very plug & play friendly. I want you to try other Micro Sales Funnels. If you come across one that sounds interesting, try it. If it doesn't work, you can always cut that

Micro Sales Funnel off and add in a new one for the same product or service.

Here are a few funnel "gurus" that you may find insightful:

- **Russell Brunson** – Founder of ClickFunnels. Has written several books on sales funnels. Has dozens of Micro Sales Funnel models, plus talks about stacking (combining) them for maximum effectiveness. He has too many products and resources to list and all of them are great, just Google him.
- **Aaron Fletcher** – Has the "Fletcher Method" and the "One Page Marketing Funnel". The Fletcher Method is an ideology behind structuring your business and creating great offers. If you're struggling with figuring out what to offer, I recommend checking out his method. His One Page Marketing Funnel is essentially a Product Launch Funnel; however, he incorporates retargeting, phone calls, and even snail mail which make it more effective. Learn more at http://fletchermethod.com/
- **Ryan Deiss** – Owns more companies than I can count and all are powered by very solid sales funnels. Like Russell Brunson, he has a lot of stuff to offer and is worth a Google search; however, what's likely most interesting to you is his Follow Up Machine. It's a similar concept to the Interest Driven Sales Funnel I teach in that it incorporates your entire business, gauges interest, etc., but he, of course, has his own spin on it. Learn more at http://followupmachine.com/backdoor
- **Todd Brown** – Another sales funnel "guru" worth checking out. He has a bunch of different Micro Sales Funnel models that he teaches, all with his unique spin. Learn more about Todd and his funnels at http://marketingfunnelautomation.com/
- **Traffic and Funnels** – A heavy focus on developing client acquisition systems, similar to the "Call / Application Funnel" I outlined above. If you offer higher end products or services that

require conversation, you may find their training to be incredibly helpful. Learn more at http://trafficandfunnels.com/

Those are just some of the people I follow with regard to sales funnels. Of course, there are many others out there and if you find someone that really resonates with you, follow them!

Combining Funnels

As if the possibilities for Micro Sales Funnels weren't already endless, in this final section, we'll briefly discuss combining them to make them even more effective!

In general, the "Classic" Sales Funnel is the perfect addition to most Product Launch and Webinar Funnels because it makes perfect sense to combine the two:

Product Launch => The "Classic"

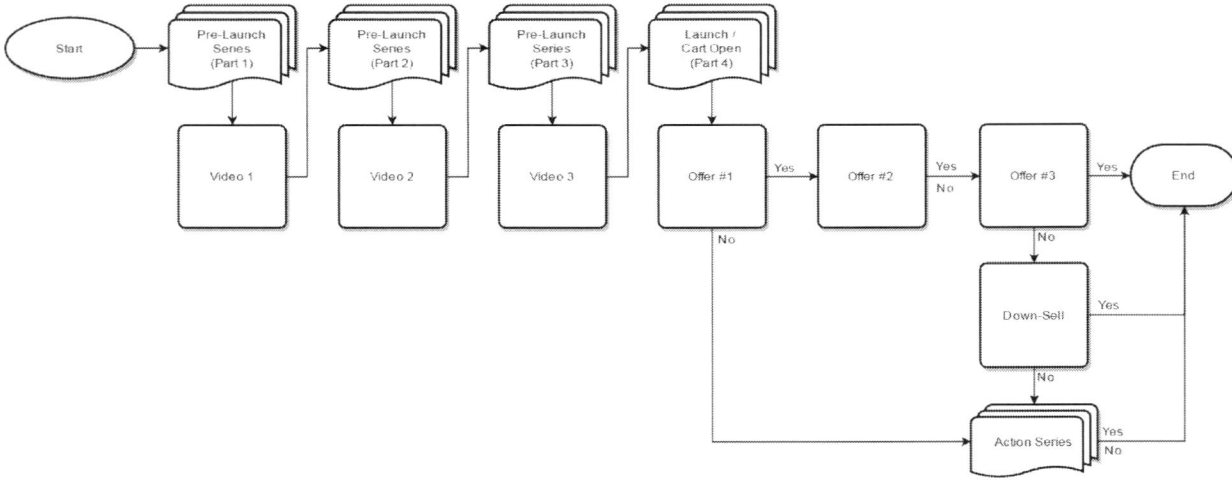

Webinar => The "Classic"

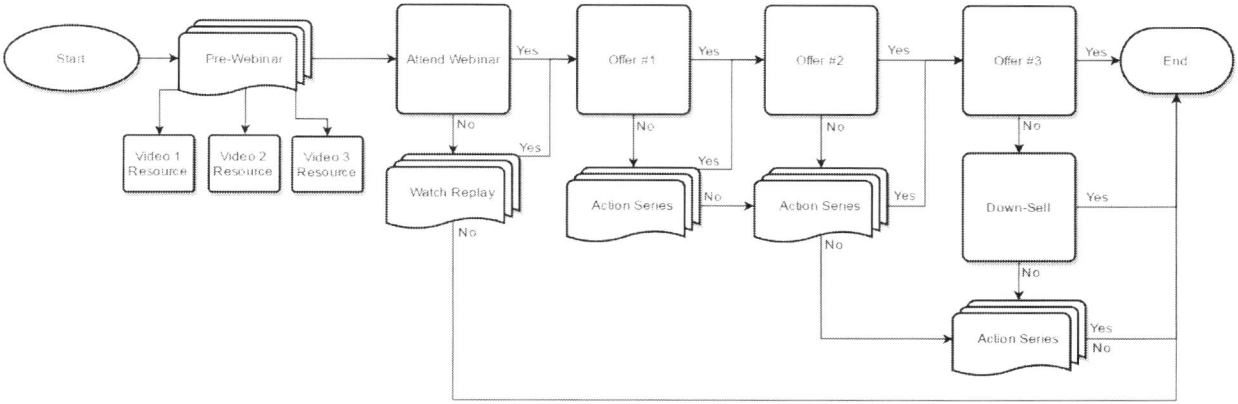

Makes sense, right? You're already making an offer and if they buy it, you simply offer more.

The "Classic" => Call / Application Funnel

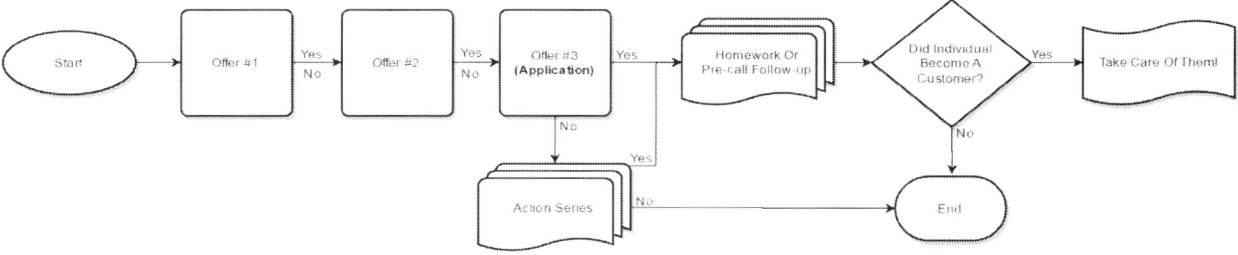

The Call / Application Funnel also fits nicely on the backend of most other funnels, especially when you're trying to get someone on the phone and/or to qualify themselves for your higher end products and services.

At the end of the day, combine funnels in ways that makes sense for what you offer. Never lose sight of your customer, their needs, and the natural path they should take through your Micro Sales Funnels.

The Content

The Content

As you can tell by now, there's a lot of writing and content creation going into these sales funnels.

Content creation includes all the emails or engagements, the sales pages or video sales letters, the product launch videos, webinars, ads, blog posts, YouTube videos, and beyond.

Even though you're not going to sit down and create all of this in one day and your Interest Driven Sales Funnel will grow over time, it's still a lot of work.

The good news is there's a methodology for all this content creation that will help guide your success.

I'm referring to **copywriting**.

If you're unfamiliar with the concept, you can find one of the best and most fun definitions for copywriting here: http://kopywritingkourse.com/what-is-copywriting/

For our sake, copywriting is the art and science of creating content, whether text, video, images, etc. that gets people to **take the action** we desire - clicking, buying, calling, subscribing, etc.

Copywriting doesn't mean creating pushy, salesy, high pressure content. It's about connecting with your customer and framing your content in a way that drives the action you desire.

By knowing copywriting is a "thing" and by having a basic understanding of how it works, you're going to look at all the content you create in a new light.

You will start creating more engaging content that leads people down a path, where by the end, they'll be excited to take whatever action you request.

While this is by no means a book on copywriting - *there are people much smarter than I that have written books on the topic* - I still wanted to take a few minutes to get you pointed in the right direction.

Having even the simplest understanding will help you tremendously.

Copywriting Formulas

Everyone loves formulas, right? All you need to do is follow them and boom! You're rich!

Ok, obviously it's not that easy, but formulas get you moving in the right direction.

Fortunately, there are hundreds of copywriting formulas to suit your every need. There are the "tried and true" formulas, some for long form copy like sales pages, others for one sentence ads, and everything in between.

These copywriting formulas work so well because they are deeply rooted in psychology. By following them, you're able to hit on certain psychological cues, or angles, that really connect with your leads and customers.

The formulas help you cover all of your bases, and ensure you don't leave anything out.

Google will be your friend here; simply Google "copywriting formulas" and start looking for one that resonates with you and the product or service you're trying to sell. Some of these formulas have massive write-ups with tons of examples, you should never feel "stuck".

A Few Popular Copywriting Formulas

Here are a few, very popular, copywriting formulas you may find helpful:

Before-After-Bridge

- **Before** – What life is like *before* your product/service enters it

- **After** – How great life is *after* your product/service is in your subscriber's life

- **Bridge** – Your product/service … aka … How to get to the "after"

Problem-Agitate-Solve

- **Problem** – Identify the problem in your subscriber's life

- **Agitate** – Make the subscriber "angrier" about their problem

- **Solve** – Present your product/service as the solution to this aggravating problem

Attention-Interest-Desire-Action (AIDA)

- **Attention** – Grab your subscriber's attention by being bold

- **Interest** – Give your subscriber interesting information on the problem your product/service solves

- **Desire** – Present the benefits of the product/service and provide proof it does what you say

- **Action** – Ask them to buy

How To Use The Formulas With Your Emails (Action Series)

As I alluded to earlier, these copywriting formulas can be used in a variety of places. You can use them to help structure your sales pages, your ads, your blog posts, and of course – your emails.

You will typically use these formulas when you write your Action Series emails. Remember, copywriting is all about getting people to take action – which is exactly what we want from our Action Series. You're no longer trying to gauge interest, you've done that via the Main Series, Specific Lead Magnet, click, pageview, etc. Now it's time to get the individual to buy something from you.

How you'll apply these formulas to your email marketing campaigns will depend on your audience and what you're trying to sell.

Some audiences enjoy receiving long, thorough emails; others want a short blurb with a link to more information.

Complex or expensive products and services tend to take more "convincing" than simple or cheaper products and may require more emails to ensure you cover all the angles.

Here are a few ways to use these powerful copywriting formulas to structure your emails:

1 Email, Short

In this scenario, include the entire copywriting formula in one email … in as few sentences as possible.

The goal is to get people to click through in order to receive more information.

This scenario comes in handy when your audience doesn't read long emails and/or mainly checks their email on a mobile device. They don't have the time to sit and scroll through a long winded email.

For example (AIDA): Missing out? 99% of small businesses don't have a sales funnel. Stop leaving money on the table! **Click Here to learn more!**

1 Email, Long

In this scenario, you would include the entire copywriting formula in one email, but it would be presented in several sentences and paragraphs – more like a sales page.

The goal is to really "sell" in the email. It can even link directly to the order form as opposed to a sales page.

This scenario comes in handy when you want to try a different angle than the normal sales page or if you're trying to sell an affiliate product. (When you don't control the sales page, but want to provide as much information as possible in your own voice before sending your subscriber to someone else's sales page, this is a good method.)

Email Series

In this scenario, you break up the copywriting formula across several emails.

The goal is to introduce different angles to the subscriber to drive them to either your sales page or order form (if it makes sense to do so).

For example, with the problem-agitate-solve formula, the first email could talk solely about the problem your subscriber is facing. The second email would agitate the problem by relating it to emotion or what they're missing out on by having this problem. The third email lays out the solution, ie. your product or service.

This scenario comes in handy when you're trying to sell something complicated and/or expensive and you need more time.

In Annex B, I've included two pre-written Action Series that follow proven copywriting formulas. These will help you better understand this concept and get you moving in the right direction!

Conclusion

Sales funnels require heaps of content. Whether digital or physical; written, video or imagery; sales pages, ads or emails – no matter the medium, it's a lot.

The good news is, if you follow the Interest Driven Sales Funnel concept, you don't need to create all the content in one day. The system you develop is modular, meaning you can add a few pieces of content to your Main Series, then work on a Micro Sales Funnel for one of your products, then add a few more pieces of content to your Main Series, and so on.

Don't let the sheer amount of content creation scare you. Let proven copywriting formulas guide your content creation. All you need to do is follow them, there's no need to reinvent the wheel each time.

Finally, it's always better to create your own content; however, you can certainly use the works of others for inspiration and guidance!

Take Action!

Now What?

Books are great.

They teach you so much nifty stuff and usually leave you feeling like you've accomplished a great task…

Then reality sets in and you realize you've produced nothing.

Would you trust a brain surgeon who has only read a book on brain surgery? Someone who hasn't at least practiced on cow brains or something?

I know I wouldn't.

Not that sales funnels are as complex as brain surgery, but they still require practice.

They still require work.

You're not going to multiply your revenue by simply consuming.

You have to take action.

Start small.

Start collecting contact information.

Start sending interest gauging content via a Main Series.

Start structuring your products and services in ways you can easily up-sell, down-sell, and cross-sell.

To help you on your way, I've put together some free training and resources at https://thesalesfunnelbook.com/start/.

If you have any questions, never hesitate to send me an email at nathan@crazyeyemarketing.com.

All the best to you and your business!

68

Annexes

ANNEX A: The Funnel Filler Strategy

The general rule for where to add new subscribers to your Interest Driven Sales Funnel:

- If you **don't** know the new subscriber's interest(s) – start them with the Main Series.
- If you **do** know their interest(s) – start them in a Micro Sales Funnel

Why wouldn't you know someone's interest upon sign-up? If your Lead Magnet is **general**. For example, a 15% off coupon to your entire store would be very general because you cannot easily tell what they're looking to buy.

However, a 15% off coupon for a cordless drill would be **specific** enough to know the person is looking at purchasing a cordless drill. They would then enter into a Micro Sales Funnel geared toward selling cordless drills.

Which brings me to my point, there are two types of Lead Magnets: General and Specific.

General Lead Magnets are great for capturing organic traffic (search, social, "free", etc.) because you may not really know what these people are interested in other than they landed on your website.

You typically offer these General Lead Magnets via an opt-in form like a lightbox, landing mat, side bar, ribbon, etc. across all pages on your site.

A Specific Lead Magnet, on the other hand, solves a specific problem, shows interest, qualifies the lead, and ultimately results in the sale of a product. They're very intentional.

You typically offer these Specific Lead Magnets via a landing page or squeeze page. A page with the sole purpose of capturing that individual's contact information in exchange for the Lead Magnet.

Because these Specific Lead Magnets are very intentional, they can serve as a great start to a Micro Sales Funnel and are perfect for paid traffic.

Using Paid Traffic

Using paid traffic is one of the best ways to fill your sales funnel. The goal, after all, is for you to be able to put $1 in and get $2+ back out. If you can consistently do that, why wouldn't you run copious amounts of paid traffic through your sales funnel?

But, here's the deal with paid traffic …

NEVER DO THIS… Run ads to your homepage or any other random page with the hopes someone will randomly opt-in or buy something! Every dollar you spend on paid traffic needs to be methodical and calculated! It needs to have a specific goal and metric to measure by. And, finally, unless you're doing some advanced retargeting techniques – **it must be supported by a Micro Sales Funnel!**

Have you ever tried paid advertising and been shocked by how "expensive" it is? Sometimes you can spend upwards of $10 per click! This may be fine if you're offering a $3,000 service. However, if you're trying to sell something for only $100, you're not going to make it, *unless* you have a Micro Sales Funnel in place that will increase the customer's value.

The Paid Traffic Oath

To affirm your commitment to always having a Micro Sales Funnel in place when running paid traffic, please raise your right hand and repeat:

"I solemnly swear that I will always have a Micro Sales Funnel in place when running paid traffic."

Good!

Now I can get off my soap box – I've worked with too many small businesses and entrepreneurs who are blowing money on ads with no objectives. I don't want it to happen to you.

To Squeeze Page

Here's the blueprint for running paid advertising campaigns:

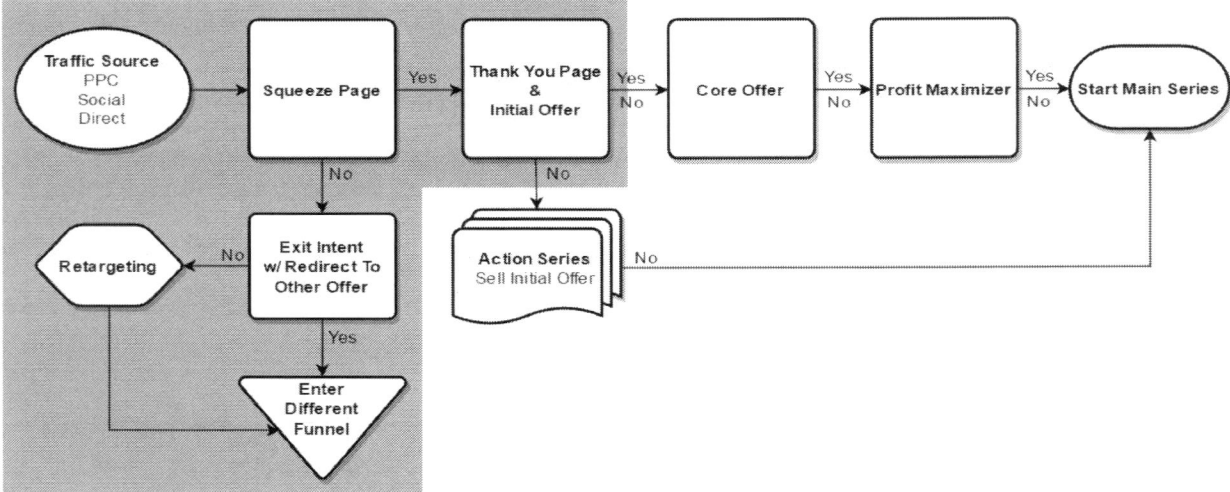

I want you to pay particularly close attention to the segment in gray because it's the start of any paid traffic campaign.

The portion not in gray is simply a Micro Sales Funnel and can look radically different depending on which one you're using. Just for reference, the one in this example is a modified version of the "Classic" Sales Funnel.

- **Traffic Source**: Where your traffic is coming from whether it's Facebook Ads, Google Adwords, Bing, or any other direct source like a banner ad.
- **Squeeze Page**: This is where you present your Specific Lead Magnet the ad was advertising and have an opt-in form so visitors can enter their contact information to receive the Lead Magnet.
- **Thank You Page & Initial Offer**: Immediately after entering their contact information, the lead should be thanked and told how to receive the Lead Magnet they just requested. Also, this is where you'll make the Initial Offer (ie. the thank you page is also a sales page).
- **Core Offer, Profit Maximizer, Action Series:** These three parts are simply the Micro Sales Funnel I'm using in this example. Yours may look radically different.
- **Start Main Series:** Since these fresh leads are new to your list – after they go through this initial Micro Sales Funnel, they join your Main Series where you begin gauging other interests and triggering other Micro Sales Funnels.

So, that covers if everything goes perfectly – the individual clicks your ad, opts-in for your Specific Lead Magnet (becomes a lead), and enters your Micro Sales Funnel where they'll hopefully become a customer.

But, what if they click your ad, land on your squeeze page, and don't opt-in?

- **Exit Intent w/ Redirect To Other Offer:** If someone lands on your squeeze page and doesn't opt-in, when they go to exit you'll have an exit-intent opt-in form appear that presents a different offer than what the squeeze page presents.

- **For example:** Let's say the squeeze page presents a Specific Lead Magnet for Facebook Ads. Unfortunately, the visitor realizes they don't want it so they decide to leave the page. As soon as their cursor leaves the browser window, we can trigger an opt-in for a different Specific Lead Magnet, one on Google Adwords. Maybe they're interested in that topic and will opt-in. If they opt-in they will …

- **Enter A Different Funnel**: Since they opted-in for the other Specific Lead Magnet, they've shown interest, and they are sent through that particular Micro Sales Funnel (ie. the sales funnel that sells our Google Adwords training).

- **Retargeting**: Sadly, sometimes people still don't opt-in to the exit-intent opt-in form. If they're on a mobile device, they won't see the opt-in form because exit-intent technology doesn't exist for mobile devices (at least not at the time of this writing). No matter the reason, the person didn't opt-in.

  But, we're not done with them yet; we still have other offers to make! These individuals are also warmer now; they've seen our brand, have an idea of what we do, and we know they're at least semi-interested in what we offer. We don't want to let them get away!

  We can run retargeting ads to the warmer leads presenting more offers until they enter one of our Micro Sales Funnels and their journey with us begins!

Just to clarify, retargeting, sometimes called remarketing, occurs when you target people with your ads based on their previous actions – ie. if they land on your squeeze page and **don't opt-in** vs. if they land on your squeeze page and **do opt-in**.

To Sales Page

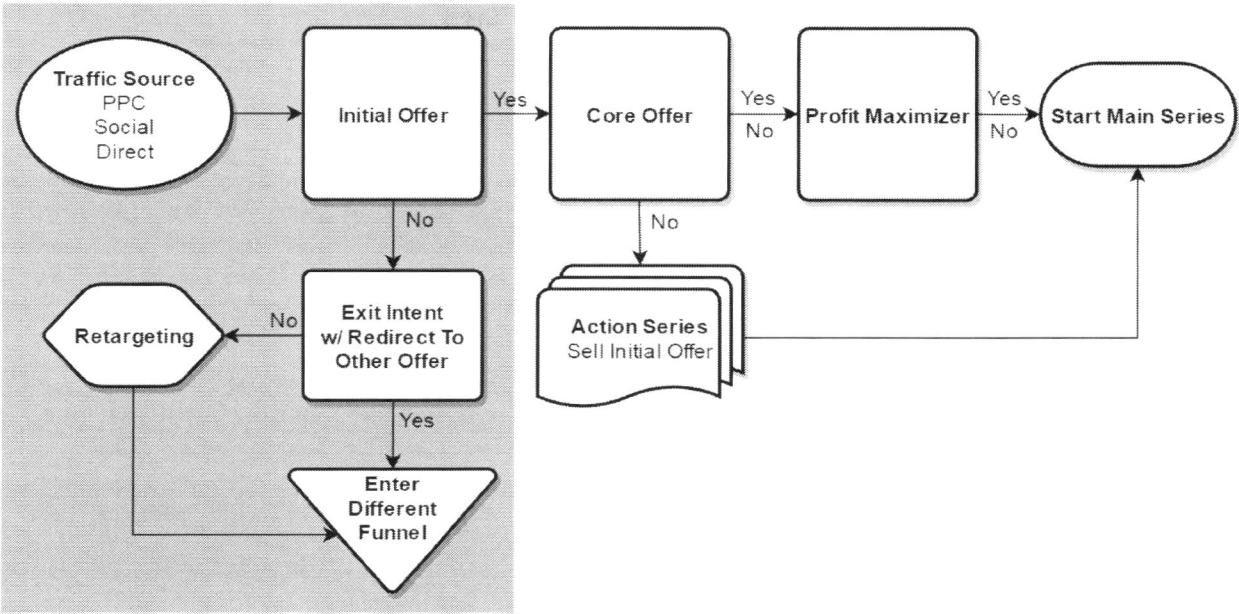

Another strategy for filling your sales funnel is to remove the squeeze page and take individuals straight to your Initial Offer.

This strategy works especially well with Free + Shipping offers – you give away something for free, like a book or a cheap product, and the customer just pays for shipping.

Other than omitting the squeeze page, the flow is the same as the previous example. I definitely recommend split-testing these two models. The results may really surprise you!

ANNEX B: Pre-written Action Series

Problem-Agitate-Solve

Email #1

Timeframe:

- Immediately or a couple hours after subscribed (if using concurrent email series)

Subject lines:

- Per your request: [lead magnet]

- Here's your download

- As you requested ... [lead magnet]

- [Symptom of problem]?

- [Problem your product/service solves]

- 99 problems but a ...

Content:

[name],

If you did not collect the name, use "Hi!" or any other saying that means "hello".

I prefer to deliver upon my promises before anything else ... so as promised, **Click here to download your copy of [lead magnet name]!**

Since you're on this email list, I know that you have a problem with [whatever problem your product/service solves].

You've spent your precious money trying to solve this problem.

Even worse ... you've wasted your time trying to solve this problem.

I know. I've *personally* been there.

And it's terrible.

This link will help solve your problem with [whatever problem your product/service solves]. [link to your sales page]

Don't delay. You know what they say - bad news gets worse with time ... as do problems.

Make it happen,

[your name]

[http://yoursite.com]

Email #2

Timeframe:

- 24 hours after Email #1

Subject lines:

- Argh! It shouldn't be this hard

- Does this bother you too?

- [Symptom of problem]?

Content:

[name].

Are you tired of [symptom of problem]?

You're not alone.

There are thousands of people trying to solve [problem your product/service solves].

People (probably even you) have tried ["Bad" solution to the problem #1], ["Bad" solution to the problem #2], and even ["Bad" solution to the problem #3].

Yet, at the end of the day all you really want is [result of your product/service].

You're tired of all the gimmicks promising X, Y, and Z.

I get it.

But, you'll **never** get past this point unless you do something about it ...

Click Here to do something about it. [link to your sales page]

Problem solved,

[your name]

[http://yoursite.com]

Email #3

Timeframe:

- 24 hours after Email #2

Subject lines:

- What's working, right now

- Did you see this?

- This works!

- [Product Name]

Content:

Ok [name],

This is *literally* it.

This product [link to your sales page] is going to solve your problems with [whatever problem your product solves].

It's *that* simple.

And ... to be honest, I'm a little astonished you're *still* having this problem.

What [product/service name] does is:

Benefit #1 - blah blah blah - Address "bad" problem #1 if possible

Benefit #2 - blah blah blah - Address "bad" problem #2 if possible

Benefit #3 - blah blah blah - Address "bad" problem #3 if possible

Remember! There is a difference between "benefits" and "features". List the BENEFITS to the end user.

- ie. Get more ladies with X

- Get more sales with X

- Don't be alone on X holiday with Y

- etc, etc, etc.

- BENEFITS!!!!

⇒ **Click Here to get more information about [product/service]**

I look forward to working with you and ... I'll talk to you later!

[your name]

[http://yoursite.com]

Features-Advantages-Benefits

Email #1

Timeframe:

- Immediately or a couple hours after subscribed (if using concurrent email series)

Subject lines:

- Per your request: [lead magnet]

- Here's your download

- As you requested … [lead magnet]

- You'll be amazed!

- By the numbers

- What is this?

Content:

Hi [name]!

If you did not collect the name, use "Hi!" or any other saying that means "hello".

I deliver upon my promises. **Please Click here to download your copy of [lead magnet name]!**

You know what's really cool?

All the things [product/service name] can do / has / consists of!

Here's a short list … *and* of course there's a LOT more; however, inboxes can only hold so much ;)

1. [Biggest feature]

2. [2nd biggest feature]

3. [3rd biggest feature]

Remember, features are distinctive attributes or facts. For example,

- Holds 1,000 songs

- 8 hour battery life

- 3.5 hours of video tutorials

- Made with handwoven bamboo

- Made in America

All of these awesome features combined result in a pretty amazing product ... if I do say so myself!

Click here to see more awesome features [link to product's sales page]

I'm excited for you!

[your name]

[http://yoursite.com]

Email #2

Timeframe:

- 24 hours after Email #1

Subject lines:

- Why we win

- Round 3. FIGHT!

- Tell us, what's easier?

Content:

[name].

Real talk.

We have some competition when it comes to [product/service name].

Competition is good. It breeds creativity and ... most importantly ... better results for you!

Right now, our #1 competitor is [name of #1 competitor].

Note: If you don't have a true "competitor" ... "fight" the status quo or what happens if they don't resolve the problem. For example, if you don't quit smoking, you may get lung cancer and die.

This is why we're better:

1. [Reason #1 why you're better]

2. [Reason #2 why you're better]

3. [Reason #3 why you're better]

For more reasons we're better and to get started, you'll want to ...

Click Here for more reasons why we have what you need! [link to sales page]

Whew, what a fight!

[your name]

[http://yoursite.com]

Email #3

Timeframe:

- 24 hours after Email #2

Subject lines:

- Achievement Unlocked!

- This is the shortcut

- 3 ways to [solve whatever problem your product/service solves]

Content:

[name]!!

I know exactly what you've been waiting for ... a *precise* list of "what we're going to do for you."

So, here it is:

1. Benefit #1

2. Benefit #2

3. Benefit #3

Remember! There is a difference between "benefits" and "features". List the <u>BENEFITS</u> to the end user.

- ie. Get more ladies with X

- Get more sales with X

- Don't be alone on X holiday with Y

- Never worry about your battery dying during the day

- Every time you wear a bamboo dress, you're saving a tree!

- etc, etc, etc.

- BENEFITS!!!!

⇒ **Click Here to get more information about [product/service]** [link to your sales page]

I look forward to working with you and ... I'll talk to you later!

[your name]

[http://yoursite.com]

ANNEX C: How To Figure Out What To Sell (Value Ladder Concept)

This is a blog post from https://crazyeyemarketing.com/blog/how-to-create-a-value-ladder-for-your-sales-funnel/. I think it will be incredibly helpful for those that are struggling to figure out what to try and sell with regard to up-sells, down-sells, and cross-sells.

How To Create A Value Ladder For Your Sales Funnel

This Is Important!

Before charging head first into sales funnel creation, you ***need*** to take the time to map out your value ladder – your products and services mapped in ascending order of value and price.

The Value Ladder

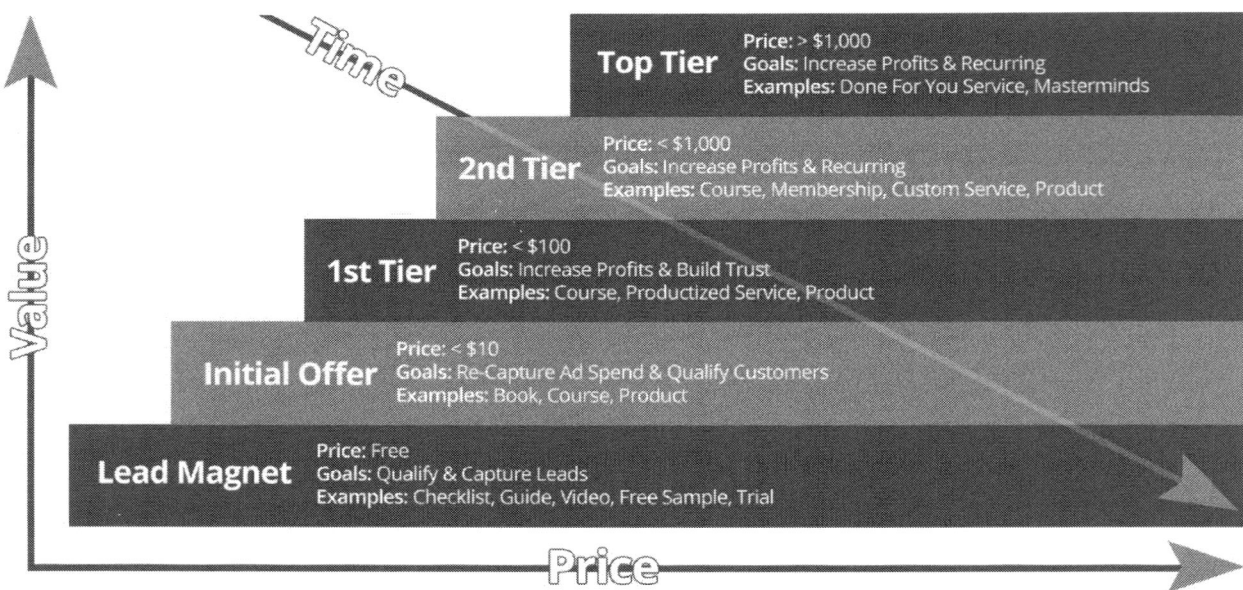

General Concept

As people "ascend" your value ladder, they're offered more value; however, this value comes at a price ($).

Note: Value doesn't necessarily mean "more". You can also provide greater value by saving people time.

Tiers

Your value ladder doesn't necessarily need 5 tiers as the diagram above shows. Offering multiple value tiers at various price points gives you more opportunity to give your customers exactly what they need.

Lead Magnet

The freebies you give away to grow your list and get people in the door.

- **Price:** Free

- **Goals:** Qualify & Capture Leads

- **Examples:** Checklist, Guide, Video, Free Sample, Trial, Coupon

Initial Offer

The low-end products you offer that ideally cover the cost of advertising and "prove" the lead has enough "pain" that they're willing to spend money to resolve it. Many times you'll see "Free plus Shipping" offers.

- **Price:** < $10
- **Goals:** Re-Capture Ad Spend & Qualify Customers
- **Examples:** Book, Course, Product

1st Tier

The low-mid range products and services you offer generate profit while simultaneously building trust with the customer as they receive more value from you and your business.

- **Price:** < $100
- **Goals:** Increase Profits & Build Trust
- **Examples:** Course, Productized Service, Product

2nd Tier

The high-mid range products and services you offer generate profit, ideally recurring revenue, from membership and continuity programs.

- **Price:** < $1,000
- **Goals:** Increase Profits & Recurring
- **Examples:** Course, Membership, Custom Service, Product

Top Tier

The biggest and best product/service you have!

- **Price:** > $1,000

- **Goals:** Increase Profits & Recurring

- **Examples:** Done For You Service, Masterminds

Product Based Businesses

I know what you're thinking, "A value ladder sounds nice, especially for digital and service based businesses, but I sell physical products and things just aren't "fitting"."

Don't worry, I've got you covered!

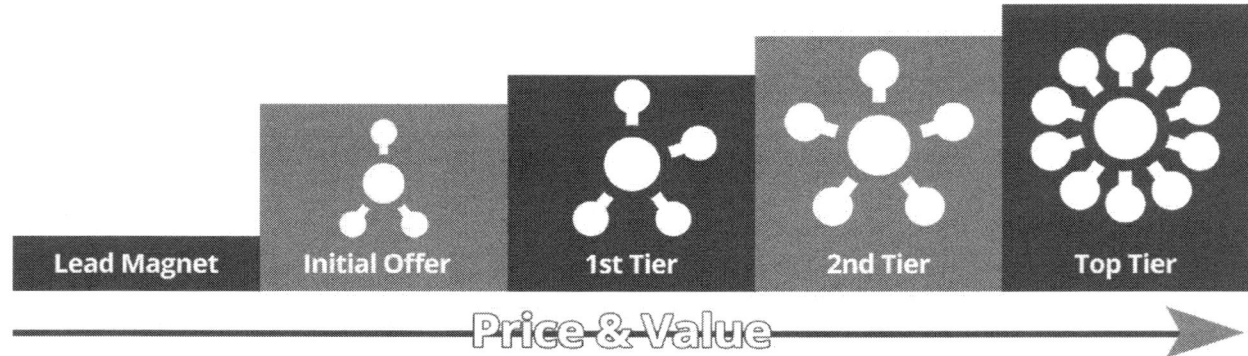

Incorporate The Hub And Spoke Model

The "hub" is the core product and the "spokes" are all the accessories and peripherals that "enhance" the core product.

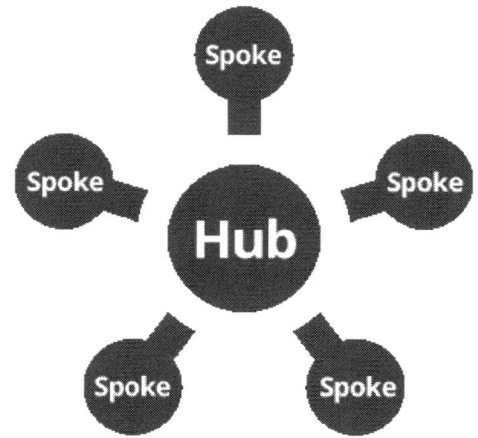

Many times, businesses that sell physical products can't "ascend" customers the same way digital and service-based businesses can.

For example, if you sell cars, you can develop and give away a lead magnet and you can likely come up with an initial offer for under $10 (ie. a car buying guide). However, after those first two steps ... there's not much ... you gotta sell a car!

You're not going to try and sell a motorized bicycle, then a scooter, then a motorcycle, then a car, then a nicer car, then an even nicer car *(at least not in one sitting)*. It simply doesn't work that way; however, after the individual purchases a car, they're going to need a lot more stuff – accessories, maintenance, insurance, credit, etc. for years to come.

The car is the "hub" and the additive products/services are the "spokes".

Eventually, *ideally*, when the individual is ready for a new car, they'll ascend to the next level, get a new car (hub), and start buying more stuff (spokes).

Another Example (Retail)

A few years ago, when I first came across the value ladder concept, I tried to apply it to an ecommerce business that also had a brick & mortar location. This particular retailer sold women's clothing – dresses, to be exact.

They offered many different types of dresses from seasonal, to professional, to formal, to wedding ... what "appeared" to be a natural ladder ... and it was, somewhat.

Many times, women would come in for a seasonal dress and leave with two or more dresses – for work and for play. However, there were many occasions where women would only need one type of dress for one specific occasion – ie. a formal occasion.

This was where the hub and spoke model came into play as there are a TON of accessories with formal wear – shoes, bags, jewelry, makeup, etc.

Let's stick with the woman that came in and purchased a formal dress. In this case, a wedding dress, even though it's "technically" the next step in the value ladder, doesn't have to be the next step ... *especially* if she's not engaged and/or doesn't have a boyfriend *(or girlfriend, whatever floats your boat – not the point).*

The point is, there are likely many seasons and occasions for more dresses (hubs) and accessories (spokes) between now and then that can be capitalized upon, if done correctly.

If it makes sense to ascend people up your ladder, ascend them. If not, be sure to incorporate enough spokes!

Offer Continuity

Often, customers will not ascend your entire value ladder *ever*, much less in one sitting. For those that do ascend, it can take weeks, months, or even years to ascend to the next level.

This is where offering a continuity program or recurring offer comes into play because it helps **accelerate ascension** while increasing **capitalization**.

For example:

- A car dealership can offer oil changes. Cars need oil changes, making this is a natural offer.

- A dress shop can offer a subscription service where every month or season they send out the appropriate style of sunglasses for maybe $10/mo. Not only will this sell more sunglasses, but it serves as a reminder to the customer that they need a new dress for the new season!

- Digital products businesses can offer a community and/or premium support as a recurring offer.

- Dentists offer 6 month check-ups.

Bundles & Down-sells

Bundles and down-sells come in handy, especially if you're stuck or are truly limited in what you have to offer.

Let's say you sell 10 different products, that all cost $30, and don't have any additional accessories, even ones you could offer as an affiliate. *(unlikely, but this is a hypothetical!)*

Could you create bundles of these products? Maybe a 3 pack, 5 pack, and 10 pack? There's your ladder!

For example:

- This concept can be applied to businesses that only offer one thing, for example, a soft serve ice cream shop. Beyond up-selling more ice cream, they can offer a punch card for $X that grants the holder 5 cups, 10 cups, 20 cups, etc. at various price breaks.

- Barber shops can also take advantage of the bundling concept. While many offer other services like shaves, dyeing, massages, etc., that can be bundled into packages, they can also bundle visits onto punch cards in a similar fashion to the ice cream shops.

- Here at Crazy Eye Marketing, we offer courses and resources individually and as a bundle we call The Vault.

Down-Sell Mega Tip!

One of the best ways to help people ascend your value ladder quickly is to reduce the entry price to the next tier.

How?

Payment plans!

Let's say your 1st Tier product costs $97 and your 2nd Tier product costs $247, you can split your 2nd Tier product into 3 easy payments of $93.67!

Doing this makes the 2nd Tier product a no-brainer as it costs less than the 1st Tier product (at least for *today* – which is what the mind tends to focus on [instant gratification]).

Reverse The Entire Ladder!

This entire time I've been talking about having customers *ascend* your value ladder, but what if you reversed it and had them *descend?!*

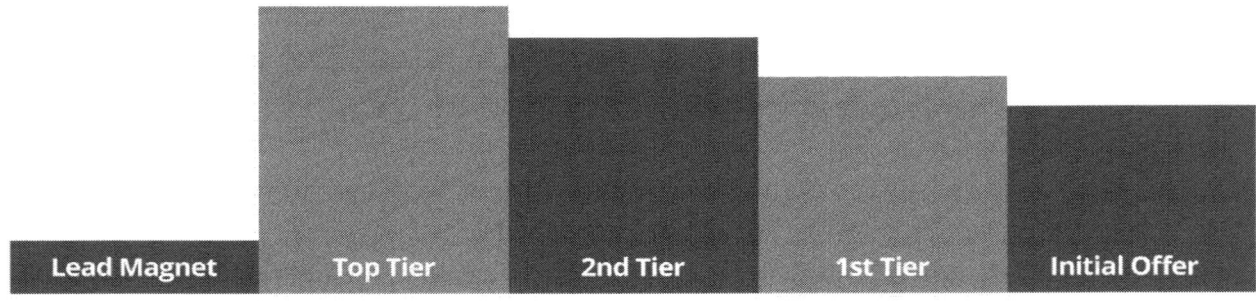

You still start with a lead magnet in order to attract and qualify leads, but then you'll go straight into presenting your top tier offer!

If they're not interested, try a "down-sell mega tip" (payment plan). If that doesn't work, move to the 2nd Tier offer. If that doesn't work, try a payment plan. If that doesn't work, move to the 1st Tier offer, and so on.

Who knows, maybe implementing a reversed value ladder will yield greater results ... it's certainly worth trying!

Printed in Great Britain
by Amazon